11/09

Langdon Public Library
328 Nimble Hill Road
Newington, NH 03801
603-436-5154
www.langdonlibrary.org

D1353906

Inc.

101
GREAT
IDEAS FOR
MANAGING
PEOPLE

from America's
Most Innovative Small Companies

EDITED BY MARTHA E. MANGELSDORF

Copyright © 1999 Goldhirsh Group, Inc.; publisher
of *Inc.* magazine
Boston, Mass.
All rights reserved.
Printed in the United States of America.

No part of this book may be used or reproduced in any
manner whatsoever without written permission from the
publisher. For information, write:
Inc. Business Resources
Attn: Permissions Manager
38 Commercial Wharf
Boston, MA 02110-3883

Editorial Director: Bradford W. Ketchum, Jr.
Managing Editor: Gail E. Anderson
Design/Production: IBR Creative Services Group

Portions of this book were originally published in *Inc.* and
Inc. Technology magazines. For information about purchasing
back issues of *Inc.* and *Inc. Technology,* please call 617-248-8426.

This publication is designed to provide accurate and
authoritative information in regard to the subject matter
covered. It is sold with the understanding that the publisher
is not engaged in rendering legal, accounting, or other
professional service. If legal advice or other expert assistance
is required, the services of a competent professional should
be sought.

**This book may be purchased in bulk at discounted rates for
sales promotions, premiums, or fund raising. Custom books
and book excerpts of this publication are available. Contact:**
***Inc.* Business Resources**
Attn: Custom Publishing Sales Dept.
38 Commercial Wharf
Boston, MA 02110-3883
1-800-394-1746

Library of Congress Catalog Number: 99-73193

ISBN 1-880394-93-6

First Edition

www.inc.com

101
GREAT IDEAS FOR MANAGING PEOPLE

CONTENTS

101
GREAT
IDEAS FOR
MANAGING
PEOPLE

• ACKNOWLEDGMENTS •

Clark Hubbard, CEO of a former *Inc.* 500 company now known as CSI Data Systems, and I were communicating through e-mail as I was working on the manuscript for this book. Hubbard closed his message by saying: "Good luck with our book. I look forward to reading it."

"*Our* book." What a great way of putting it! I suspect that all manuscripts are acts of collaboration, but this book, in particular, belongs to many people, especially the entrepreneurs like Hubbard, whose companies are featured in these pages. I thank them for their insights and for the time and energy they devoted to making sure the material is up-to-date and accurate.

Then there are the talented writers who wrote the stories in *Inc.* magazine from which the majority of these 101 great ideas are drawn. They include: Marc Ballon, Alessandra Bianchi, Bo Burlingham, Christopher Caggiano, John Case, Donna Fenn, Jay Finegan, Jill Andresky Fraser, Susan Greco, John Grossmann, Stephanie Gruner, Mike Hofman, John Kerr, Robert Mamis, Shane McLaughlin, Ilan Mochari, Sarah Schafer, Ellyn Spragins, Jerry Useem, and Edward O. Welles. For their efforts—and the efforts of the many talented people who toil behind the scenes to produce an excellent magazine—I am deeply grateful.

Next are the folks at *Inc.* Business Resources: Jan Spiro, product director; Brad Ketchum, Jr., IBR editorial director; Gail Anderson, managing editor; Audra Mulhearn, copy editor; Lynette Haggard, creative services director; Martha Abdella, graphic designer; Kevin Levesque, production artist; Kimberly Weiss, creative services traffic manager; and Simeon Ketchum, researcher. Special thanks to Brad for his wisdom and to Gail for all her hard work shepherding this project through to completion.

No book based primarily on material from the "Hands On" section of *Inc.* would be complete without a thank-you to George Gendron, *Inc.*'s longtime editor-in-chief, on whose watch that section debuted during the 1980s.

Finally, I thank the many people who helped me grow and develop, first as a small-business writer and then as an editor. A few deserve special mention: Bo Burlingham, *Inc.*'s former executive editor and my longtime mentor; Nancy Lyons, an *Inc.* senior editor with a terrific focus on how-to material that truly serves small business; and Michael Hopkins, *Inc.*'s executive editor and a great human being. Special gratitude also to Leslie Brokaw, most recently editor of Inc. Online. Leslie and I arrived at *Inc.* in 1987 as reporter/researchers, and it was fun rising through the ranks together.

Last of all, I thank the many entrepreneurs I worked with in my part-time capacity as director of high-tech programs at the nonprofit Cambridge Business Development Center (CBDC), in Cambridge, Mass., which, like *Inc.*, helps entrepreneurs grow successful businesses. And I am especially grateful to Diane Franklin, CBDC's executive director, for allowing me to "flex my flextime" as I worked on this project.

—*Martha E. Mangelsdorf*
Boston, Mass.

Editor's note: *Now a senior content producer for inc.com, Martha E. Mangelsdorf formerly served as the magazine's senior editor in charge of "Hands On," a section devoted to how-to management material. She also served as an associate editor and senior writer at* Inc. *for more than six years.*

I

"As one CEO told me, 'My bad hire was the third choice after two others were not hired. I compromised because the search was taking inordinately long. Now I know that no hire is better than a bad hire.' "

DR. PIERRE MORNELL
psychiatrist, consultant, and author of *Hiring Smart!*
How to Predict Winners and Losers in the Incredibly
Expensive People-Reading Game
(Ten Speed Press)

RECRUITING • RECRUITING • RECRUITING

1
IDEA

Off the Beaten Path

Forget the want ads. Other forms of advertising can pull, too. Ira Patton, CEO of Patton General Contracting, advertises for help on television. To recruit for his $11.1-million residential remodeling company in Charleston, S.C., Patton uses TV ads that include an 800 number. "It gets good people—the ones that already have jobs who aren't looking through the classifieds," he says. The do-it-yourself production for a 60-second ad cost Patton about $500.

Patton isn't the only entrepreneur to **get good results from nontraditional help-wanted advertising**. Michael Pehl, CEO of i-Cube, a Cambridge Mass., information technology consulting company with 1998 revenues of $41.2 million, ran a series of large billboard ads in the Boston area. One billboard, for example, targeted drivers exiting from Boston's airport with the immodest message that i-Cube is "An Incredible Place to Work." Even at a cost of $10,000 to $15,000 per month (including design fees), Pehl views the billboards as quite a bargain. "We'd pay the same thing to run a tiny one-day ad in the *Boston Sunday Globe*," he says, "but the billboard sits there for 30 days."

2
IDEA

Direct Approach

Everyone knows about direct-mail marketing, but **using direct mail to recruit employees** can work, too. Richard McCarty, a principal at McCarty Architects, a 25-employee company in Tupelo, Miss., faced the problem of attracting architects to rural Mississippi. He got good results with a lively direct-mail recruiting package sent nationwide to chapters of the American Institute of Architects. "It's hard to get people fired up about Tupelo," McCarty says. "We try to throw in something that will catch someone's eye and give an indication of the spirit of our firm and our community."

Before entering a new retail market, Select Comfort, a Minneapolis manufacturer of high-quality air mattresses, sends recruitment postcards to "Comfort Club" members—customers who have spent at least $1,200 on its innovative "sleep system." Select Comfort solicits customers to become employees because the company has found that satisfied customers make effective salespeople. "We knew if we had converts to what we were doing, we could train them in the selling process," said Mark de Naray, board member and former CEO.

Karen McFarland is a good example. As a potential customer, she was skeptical of Select Comfort's claims. (Her husband, who suffers from a degenerative spinal ailment, ordered his mattress in secret using a neighbor's phone.) Now she believes the mattress saved her husband from surgery. McFarland's enthusiasm for the product persuaded area sales manager Tim Brasfield to hire her to manage the Cary, N.C., store. He was glad he did: Her store exceeded its sales goals for 11 of 12 months, earning it three top-performance ratings.

3

IDEA

No Casual References

Many companies offer "referral bonuses" to employees for recommending job candidates who ultimately join the company. But some companies have discovered **ways to get more value from the referral bonuses they pay**.

Brett Brewster, CEO of Mitec Controls, a company that sells, services, and inspects fire alarm systems, wants to be sure that his 93 employees are thinking long-term when they refer prospects. So Brewster spreads out the bonus payments. The employee gets half of the bonus after the referral has worked at Mitec for 90 days and the rest when the referred employee passes the six-month mark. To further encourage accountability, Brewster, whose Norcross, Ga., company had 1998 revenues of $6.5 million, requires that employees spend time orienting the new hires they refer.

In another referral bonus twist, Kris Zaepfel, director of human resources for Exchange Applications, an information technology company in Boston, has set up a tiered referral program that gives employees more money for more valuable referrals. Zaepfel offers a $3,000 bonus for most positions, but she will pay $5,000 for "hot jobs" that she needs to fill with particular urgency.

Niche Networking

Recruiting in tough labor markets requires innovative approaches. One strategy is to **find specialized recruiting niches in the same way that companies develop niche markets** for their products and services. For example, you can:

➤ *Hire customers.* Black Diamond Equipment Ltd., in Salt Lake City, tries to keep ahead of its rivals in the trendy rock-climbing and backcountry-skiing equipment industry by hiring people who use its products. The company fills its workforce with outdoor sports enthusiasts and capitalizes on their passion.

"We breathe it, live it, think about it constantly," says human-resources vice-president Meredith Saarinen, "which makes the whole company a marketing and design resource. It kills complacency." Saarinen estimates that more than half of the company's 230 to 240 employees were customers before they joined Black Diamond. And that, Saarinen believes, makes for a committed workforce. "It's not that our employees *can* make suggestions," she adds, "but that they have the duty to make them…Their lives are going to be dangling from the piece of equipment they just made."

From a manager's standpoint, it's easier to promote your company as a place to work to a potential employee who already knows and likes your product. Saarinen says that Black Diamond Equipment regularly receives applications from customers who say, in effect, "This is a cool company. Got any work?"

➤ *Recruit senior citizens.* At John Greene's executive chauffeur service, CTS International, in Braintree, Mass., about 30% of the *(Continued)*

(Continued from page 15)

company's 250 employees are retirees. Greene, whose company has annual revenues of $12 million, sends letters to human-resources departments at local companies, seeking soon-to-be retirees looking for extra income.

   ɐ *Ask employees to help recruit.* David Riordan, co-owner of OOP!, a specialty-gift store in Providence with annual revenues of $1 million, knows he'll lose a good chunk of his employee base every May. That's because half his workers are students from local universities. "Even if they're great, we have them only for two to four years," he says. So when they come on board, he asks his employees to agree to find and train their replacements when they leave. This technique satisfies most of Riordan's hiring needs; he says that even though the store has been in business for 10 years, he has never had to place a help-wanted ad in the newspaper.

   ɐ *Use employee networks.* You don't have to wait until employees leave to use them as recruiting resources. Marilyn Konigsberg and Janie Murow, co-owners of MJ Java, an Omaha coffee retailer with nearly $1 million in annual sales, have had good luck hiring college students who play in bands for entry-level jobs at MJ Java. Those students make great workers, Konigsberg and Murow report, because they have a network—the music scene—from which they can refer other potential employees. As a bonus, the students excel at getting coworkers to substitute for them. "Since they have outside interests in common, they're more inclined to cover for each other," says Murow.

Howard Getson, CEO of IntellAgent Control, a software-development company in Dallas, also benefited from employee networking. When Getson hired four Baptist ministers as key programmers for his 20-employee company, it turned out to be a blessing in disguise. Since then, each minister has recruited several members of his congregation to the company. Such networking, says Getson, "has created an unparalleled atmosphere of kindness and integrity."

5
IDEA

Big Guys on Campus

On-campus recruiting isn't just for big companies. But entrepreneurs trying to recruit at colleges and universities often must contend with low recognition by students and lack of interest by the administration. Here's how two companies **increase their presence during on-campus recruiting**.

When Lloyd Shefsky, a founding partner of Shefsky & Froelich Ltd., needed young hires for his Chicago-based law firm, which has about 30 partners, he called his alma mater. Shefsky offered to be a guest lecturer at his former law professors' classes, and the professors agreed. With the credibility provided by his alma mater, Shefsky soon was making the rounds at other law schools. And once his firm became known on campuses, he found it easier to recruit top students.

Meanwhile, Doug Evans, president of Doug Evans + Partners, an eight-employee consulting firm in New York City, found that a bit of chutzpah helped him recruit newly minted M.B.A.s, who typically set their sights on *Fortune* 500 companies. When Evans first approached one prestigious business school, he says the administration wouldn't even talk to him. When it finally responded, all he got was a tiny room in which to pitch his Internet, e-commerce, and technology company to prospective hires.

Undaunted, Evans took a different approach to achieve a larger on-campus presence. He called a client who was a graduate of the school, and that client helped Evans get the pricey-but-prime suite where companies such as Arthur Andersen made their presentations. Evans also networked with on-campus organizations, and he inundated candidates *(Continued)*

(Continued from page 17)

with e-mails, direct mail, and telephone calls to maximize attendance. The result? His presentation at that school yielded three new employees.

Even if you don't host a big on-campus presentation, the Internet can help you recruit at colleges. Ask John Coleman, CEO of Via Marketing & Design, a marketing and communications company based in Portland, Maine. Coleman, whose fast-growing company projects $10 million to $12 million in revenues for 1999, posted a listing for a senior marketing strategist at the Harvard Business School's Web site. He received a few dozen responses, from which he hired Chris Lane, a former White House aide with an accomplished career in marketing. Coleman says Lane was one of his best hires, and the price of recruiting (free) was certainly reasonable.

Coleman also spent some money—$5,000 for a service called University ProNet (www.universitypronet.com)—that he says turned out to be a good deal. The site wields a hefty database that tracks the personal and professional information of 131,000 alumni from such top-tier schools as Stanford and Carnegie Mellon. Coleman says he's had about the same success with ProNet as with conventional headhunters, minus one key factor—the headhunters' fee, which could amount to several tens of thousands of dollars.

6
IDEA

Train 'Em, Retain 'Em

Steve Burkhart, CEO of Advanced Micro-Electronics (AME), used to get frustrated trying to find qualified job candidates for his PC-maintenance and networking company, which is based in Vincennes, Ind. So in 1990, when his company had $1.6 million in sales and 43 employees, Burkhart approached a local junior college, Vincennes University. He worked with Vincennes faculty to create a computer-repair program designed around the needs of companies like AME. "We tell Vincennes about the newest, handiest thing," says Burkhart, "and they adapt their program to meet that need."

Vincennes students trained under this program comprise a pool of talent from which Burkhart often recruits full-time employees. In 1998, more than 50 of AME's 150 employees were Vincennes graduates—including not just technical employees but also managerial and administrative staff. "To us, Vincennes is like a garden," he says. "We nurture it, and it produces fruit."

Large companies have been involved in such **"school-to-work" relationships** for quite some time. But increasing numbers of small companies are entering partnerships with local high schools and colleges, notes Peter Cappelli, professor of management at the Wharton School at the University of Pennsylvania, in Philadelphia. These relationships can benefit the schools as well as the businesses. Dean Ackerman, a professor of electronics at Vincennes University, says AME has much to offer him and his students. For example, Ackerman trains with AME's technicians to stay current on the latest technology.

7
IDEA

Don't Wait 'til They Graduate

Ask small-business owners for a list of management woes, and the lack of skilled workers is likely to be near the top. An increasing number of companies, such as Jet Products, in Phoenix, are taking steps to address that problem.

Over a 10-year period, Jet, a precision-machining facility which has annual revenues of $7 million, has **apprenticed nearly 50 students**, mostly high-school seniors recruited through the local school district's cooperative education program. Apprentices are paid $6 an hour for a 20-hour workweek that includes operating shop-floor machinery, as well as formal classroom training from Jet's team leaders. The students work after school four days a week, from 4 p.m. to 9 p.m.

According to Jet vice-president Jim Perlow, Jet's apprenticeship program not only gives the company the opportunity to screen and train future workers (about 20 apprentices are still with Jet, now as full-time employees) but also provides students with a real-world context for what they're studying in school. "Once they're in the work world," says Perlow, "they see the reason for continuing their education."

If the students' grades are up to par and Jet hires them full time, the company will pay all future education costs toward an associate's degree in manufacturing technology. In fact, that education benefit extends to all full-time employees. "We're trying to teach them that education is a continuous process," he notes.

"We're better positioned in the marketplace because our employees are younger, more easily motivated, and better educated," says Perlow. "Right now, our strength is in all these young people."

8

IDEA

Cut to the Chase

In a tight labor market, it pays to act quickly. In April 1997, a programmer posted her curriculum vitae to the Web site of Statprobe, an $11-million drug-trial research company based in Ann Arbor, Mich. She explained that she was looking for a job because her current employer, one of Statprobe's competitors, was closing its office in Lexington, Ky., at the end of June. By July 1, Statprobe had opened an office in Lexington—and staffed it with 50 of the competitor's former employees.

In Statprobe's industry, competition for talent has been fierce. "If we can find the right people, we'll set up an office for them," notes Statprobe president Lora Schwab. Schwab's 10-year-old company, which projects 1999 revenues of $23 million, has six offices nationwide and has made the *Inc.* 500 list of the fastest-growing privately held U.S. companies.

Some entrepreneurs **target competitors' employees** even more aggressively. When Barry Brodersen, cofounder and vice-president of Domino Equipment Co., in Clinton, Okla., hears about a particularly good service or construction specialist, he tries to get as much information about that person as he can and looks for opportunities to become acquainted. Once, Brodersen *literally* pursued a service specialist he had heard about by tailgating him for 30 miles. When the two vehicles finally stopped, Brodersen introduced himself and said, "Why don't you come work for me?" Now the man is a service manager for Brodersen, whose company installs and services petroleum equipment.

9
IDEA

Making the Team

For Joe Lethert Sr., the use of temporary employees yields permanent recruiting results. Lethert, the president of Performark, a relationship-marketing agency in Bloomington, Minn., estimates that two-thirds of Performark's full-time employees began as temps.

"It has been the best source of new people we have," he says. Performark, which had 1998 sales of $12 million, has 150 employees, about 25% of them temporary. Using temps regularly, Lethert says, helps his company manage a fluctuating workload without laying off permanent employees. And by **recruiting from its base of temporary workers**, Lethert notes, Performark can make permanent hiring decisions after seeing how a person performs.

To get the most benefits from its temporary workforce, Performark takes its temps seriously. Temporary workers are screened as thoroughly as prospective permanent employees, and once on board, temps go through the same training and orientation as other employees. Temps at Performark are also eligible for incentives and bonuses. For instance, everyone at the company's 85-person call center competes for daily prizes, such as movie tickets and pizza lunches. Temporary workers attend the six annual company outings, including the annual awards dinner and dance.

"You can't expect the same performance from temporary employees that you get from full-time workers if you don't treat them the same way," Lethert observes. "The key is to have the mindset that these are employees."

Flexible High Flyer

Would you like to lure big-time executive talent to your company? Do you worry that you can't afford to pay the kind of salaries big companies offer? Sometimes **flexibility is the key to executive recruiting success**. Just ask Clark Hubbard, the CEO of $10-million CSI Data Systems, a value-added computer reseller based in Norcross, Ga. In 1995, Hubbard desperately needed the expertise of a chief financial officer (CFO) before his company could quite afford it. Back then, Hubbard's company, which had about $4 million in annual sales, experienced some serious inventory control problems. "I needed somebody to come in from the outside and examine all our financial operations to figure out what was happening and how to stop it quickly," Hubbard recalls.

Hubbard had the perfect candidate in mind: a friend who had worked for years as the CFO of a multinational corporation, only to lose his job after a merger. "He was extremely overqualified and way too expensive for us, but I trusted him completely. And he needed some work," Hubbard explains. "I told him, 'I sure as hell can't afford you, but if you'll accept the salary I can pay and give us top priority, I'll let you take on additional clients and meet with them at our offices.'"

The friend accepted the arrangement—and then revamped CSI's financial system, upgraded its accounting software, and solved the inventory control problem. "He set up a cash-management system for us so that extra funds get swept into an investment account each night," says Hubbard. "He also helped us establish a line of bank credit, which we'd never had before. Those two changes alone accomplished wonders   *(Continued)*

(Continued from page 23)

on the cash-flow front and really helped us double our business in just a year."

In fact, Hubbard's company grew so quickly that, in 1996, it made the *Inc.* 500 list of the fastest-growing privately held U.S. companies. (At the time, the company was known as Computer Stuff) As for the CFO, Hubbard acknowledges he would have "probably never even thought about making the hire if the inventory crisis hadn't happened." However, when that first CFO left for a better-paying job, Hubbard promptly hired a replacement. In fact, the first CFO even recruited his successor—and "gave him the highest of recommendations," Hubbard says. "It just so happened that the replacement was his brother, also a friend of mine whom I had known for years." Admittedly, this was an unusual arrangement, but Hubbard notes jokingly that it had unexpected benefits. "Since they both had the same last name, we didn't even have to replace the nameplates on the CFO's door."

"What you ask during an interview is not nearly as important as how you listen."

JANE WESMAN
founder and president,
Jane Wesman Public Relations, and author of
Dive Right In—the Sharks Won't Bite
(Prentice Hall)

Law of Averages

I t's a classic problem. As your company grows, it becomes more difficult to maintain hiring standards—particularly when you no longer do all the hiring yourself. Jim Koch, founder of Boston Beer Co., faced that problem while growing the Boston-based business from a start-up to a company with approximately 300 employees. Koch found that it helps to have a simple hiring rule, "so people can understand and visualize and don't have to try to imagine what you mean."

Koch's rule: **Don't hire anybody unless it improves the average of the company.** "It's a wonderful rule because administrators can imagine what the average person is like; there's a fairly clear standard in their heads," Koch explains. "They look at this person and they can say, 'Yeah, they're better,' or more likely, 'No, they're not better than our average.'"

Why is the rule so important? "When you start on a scale of 1 to 10," explains Koch, "you hire 8s and 9s and 10s. Then you start hiring 7s, and the 7s hire 6s, and the 6s start hiring 4s and 5s. And before you know it, what started out as 8s, 9s, and 10s are 4s, 5s, and 6s on their way to becoming 1s and 2s and 3s."

12

IDEA

Guerrilla Hiring

Think you have problems finding good people? In 1998, Roger Mody, CEO of Signal Corp., described unemployment in his industry (information-technology services) as "practically nonexistent." Yet Signal, an *Inc.* 500 company that is based in Fairfax, Va., grew from $4.2 million in sales and 58 employees in 1992 to sales of $146 million and 1,325 employees by the end of 1998. The company's explosive growth occurred despite a tight labor market during that period. Instead of letting the labor market stunt his company's growth, however, Mody developed **new strategies to interview and hire more efficiently**. His methods include:

☙ *Interview during off-hours.* Signal began conducting most job interviews before or after work hours or on weekends, because those times are more convenient for many job candidates. "When people interview during work hours, they're usually stressed because they're not where they're supposed to be," Mody observes. Signal does, however, accommodate candidates who prefer to interview during the day.

☙ *Stagger human-resources shifts.* With an unconventional interviewing schedule, Mody realized that Signal's human-resources people could not work conventional hours, so the company runs staggered human-resources shifts. Some HR people start at 7 a.m., and a second shift starts later in the morning. The result: Thirteen hours of HR coverage each day. "If we want to make a job applicant an offer at 8 p.m., we have the staff available to do it," Mody says. "That scheduling also helps us take care of our West Coast employees."

☙ *Use high-level people to conduct interviews.* "We want   *(Continued)*

(Continued from page 27)

to attract the kind of new employees our customers will think highly of," Mody explains. "But the pace of our recruiting is so rapid that we don't have the luxury of putting candidates through three levels of screening." Mody's solution: He gets the company's operating vice-presidents involved in the early stages of the interview process. Having them conduct the first interview is a considerable time-saver, Mody says. "They know exactly what they're looking for," he observes. "They go right for the jugular and ask tough technical questions."

• *Establish internal recruiting deadlines.* Mody discovered that his company wasn't making recruiting decisions as quickly as some of his competitors. "If it took us two weeks to get back to the candidates, they were gone," he recalls. So Signal established a recruiting timeframe, and managers aim to adhere to it. For example, when a Signal manager receives a résumé in response to an opening, he or she has a day and a half to decide whether to schedule an interview.

• *Look at candidates' long-term potential.* "Even if we don't hire folks now, we want them to have a favorable opinion of our company should they go on to acquire the necessary skills," Mody says. So Signal tries to respect candidates' time. Before someone arrives for an interview, Signal employees fill out any information they already know on the application form—such as name and address. "It's a small gesture of respect," he notes. "But you can't imagine the number of candidates who respond to it with positive comments."

IDEA 13

Screening Room

Do you find screening and interviewing job candidates an overwhelming time drain? Keith Alper, president of Creative Producers Group, in St. Louis, uses an interviewing method that **screens as many as a dozen promising candidates in less than two hours**. Potential hires at the 40-employee corporate communications agency are invited to a 20-minute presentation about the company, followed by a question-and-answer period. Then, each candidate meets with a senior staff member for five to seven minutes. The strongest candidates are invited back for more in-depth interviews. The other candidates, Alper claims, generally appreciate not having wasted a lot of time.

This group interview method serves a number of functions. "It lets us have a feel for all the candidates in one room," says Alper. A few participants disqualify themselves right away by being late or asking inane questions, he reports. The company's managers also get a chance to observe the candidates interacting with one another. Finally, the group presentation saves the company significant amounts of time.

REAL
WORLD

"We look for people who want to win every situation they approach."

PATRICK KELLY
founder and CEO,
PSS/World Medical, Jacksonville, Fla.,
and author, with John Case, of
*Faster Company: Building the World's
Nuttiest Turn-on-a-Dime, Home-Grown,
Billion-Dollar Business*
(John Wiley & Sons)

Grilled to Order

Bad hiring decisions can cost a company big money, so it pays to fine-tune your interviewing techniques. Many smart managers are developing their own **idiosyncratic interview questions tailored specifically to their organization's culture**. For example, Jim Sheward, CEO of Fiberlink, a Blue Bell, Pa., Internet consulting company with annual revenues of $10 million, places a lot of stock in his staff's integrity. So his favorite question to ask interviewees is, "What's the biggest career mistake you've made so far?" Sheward looks for reflective candidates who have learned from their errors. "I've found that those who can't think of anything either don't take risks or aren't telling me the truth," he says.

Of course, some questions are just plain practical. Tired of making offers to folks who had already accepted *other* offers, Eric Schechter, CEO of Great American Events, an event-marketing and merchandising company in Scottsdale, Ariz., that projects 1999 revenues of $3.5 million, asks the following: "Who else are you interviewing with, and how close are you to accepting an offer?"

Here's a sampling of what other small-company owners and managers ask job candidates—and why.

&. *John Discerni*, CEO, Physicians Formulary International, a wholesale pharmaceutical company in Phoenix with 1998 revenues of $18 million.

What he asks: "What's the last book you've read?"

Why: Discerni says that it's not what they read so much as the amount of time it takes for them to answer the question: If they have to think a long time, they probably aren't that well read. *(Continued)*

(Continued from page 31)

&. *Tony Petrucciani*, CEO, Single Source Systems, a systems integration company in Fishers, Ind., with 1998 revenues of $6.5 million.

What he asks: "Why do they make manhole covers round?"

Why: "We ask this of potential developers to see if they get flustered, and how they think on their feet," says Petrucciani. (The answer: Because covers of any other simple geometric shape could fall through.)

&. *Robert Baden*, CEO and president, Rochester Software Associates, a software developer in Rochester, N.Y., with 1998 revenues of $5 million.

What he asks: "If I stood you next to a skyscraper and gave you a barometer, how could you figure out how tall the building was?"

Why: The answer: Well, there really isn't one. Baden just wants to see how creative people are. According to company lore, one interviewee responded that he'd find the building's janitor and then offer the janitor the barometer in exchange for information about the building's height.

&. *Doug Chapiewsky*, CEO and president, CenterPoint Solutions, a software developer in Denver with 1998 revenues of $2.5 million.

What he asks: "If you had your own company, what would it do?"

Why: "I want to see if they've got that certain entrepreneurial spirit it takes to succeed in a small software company," he says.

&. *Madonna Flanders*, employment manager, Community Health and Counseling Services, a mental-health and home-health services company with more than 1,000 employees, based in Bangor, Maine.

What she asks: "If I asked your previous coworkers for key words to describe you, what would they say? Then if I leaned close and whispered, 'Now tell me what I'd better watch out for,' what would they say?"

Why: To find out how in touch candidates are with their strengths and weaknesses. "I also get information that I can check with references when I call," says Flanders.

IDEA

A Leading Question

Money and benefits are the usual carrots dangled before potential employees. But sometimes they are ridiculously inappropriate, and it's important to understand each person's motivation. To illustrate the point, Ron Parks, president of Millard Manufacturing, a stainless steel fabricator and distributor in Omaha, poses this question: What manager would have been able to motivate Mother Teresa with a retirement plan?

After nearly 30 years of managing experience, Parks has devised **an interviewing technique to figure out what motivates an individual**. The information helps Parks select the right person for a job at his 60-employee company, but it's also an invaluable management tool.

To pinpoint a person's source of motivation, he asks, "When you are working on a project, how do you know you are doing a good job?" People who tell you that they know within themselves whether their work is first-rate are, in Parks's term, "internal" or self-directed. Those who say, "My boss (or my coworkers) tells me so," are external, requiring input from the outside.

Either may be a desirable worker in the right job. Obviously, externals would flounder in positions in which their work is rarely reviewed. Nor would they thrive working for a boss who is stingy with praise.

In contrast, praise is sometimes not the best tool with the self-directed. Such people will feel embarrassed, or even offended, if complimented by someone unqualified to judge their accomplishments, Parks notes.

Parks, who has spent decades perfecting his "thinking model" of management, asks another dozen or so questions to ascertain an employee's performance profile. But if he could focus on one trait only, Parks would choose motivation.

Remote Possibilities

More and more companies are operating virtually—that is, using technology to link workers in remote locations. But when you're hiring, how do you **identify the candidates best suited to a virtual environment**?

Will Pape, cofounder of VeriFone, has given that question a lot of thought because for many years he served as chief information officer at the self-described "virtual company," which makes electronic payment systems. (VeriFone, which is based in Santa Clara, Calif., has since been acquired by Hewlett-Packard.) Some of the characteristics Pape learned to look for when hiring virtual workers are listed below. He does advise, however, that "not every successful virtual worker has each characteristic, that most of the skills can be learned, at least to some degree, and that a company's practices can compensate for shortfalls."

☞ *Does the candidate have strong communication skills?* "Virtual workers don't have the luxury of communicating face-to-face, which means they miss out on nonverbal as well as verbal cues. It also means they have to communicate both their point of view and personality through media such as videoconferencing, e-mail, or the telephone," Pape notes. "They need strong verbal and written skills—skills that you can assess early in the hiring process by speaking to candidates on the phone or communicating via e-mail."

☞ *Does he or she take the initiative in communication?* "Staff members who wait to be asked, who don't take the initiative to inform, are going to lower productivity," Pape observes. "You want people who won't hesitate to make that phone call or send that e-mail. Ask references, especially past supervisors, about candidates' willingness to open the channels of communication."

How good is the candidate at solving problems independently? "When workers are out of sight, managers may not know which people are thrashing around unproductively on a problem," Pape notes. "Employees have to be able to tackle problems head-on, generate and implement solutions independently, and ask for help when they get stuck."

A good way to find out about candidates' problem-solving skills is to ask them to describe how they solved difficult problems. Have them focus on specific things they said or did. Then ask if they feel comfortable tackling problems on their own. You can help remote workers improve problem-solving skills, suggests Pape, by having them do short (10- to 15-minute) problem-solving exercises. And you can reinforce problem-solving capabilities by circulating success stories about individual employees or groups that have done a great job dealing with one problem or another.

How loyal will the candidate be? "Because virtual workers don't have everyday face-to-face interaction with fellow employees, their personal and company ties can be weaker than those of workers in the traditional organization," says Pape. That, he notes, can lead to higher turnover, which is a drain on a business's productivity. "Look for employees who have demonstrated their loyalty to a company (workers with longevity and ones with strong reasons for changing jobs) and who believe in the goals and values of your company," Pape suggests. "Testing for congruity with your company's goals and values can be as simple as asking candidates to describe their ideal company."

How strong is his or her work ethic? "Look for people who show a quick understanding of what needs to be done, who stay on task and deliver results, not excuses," says Pape. "Ask for examples from both the applicants and their references."

How secure is the candidate about his or her ability?   (Continued)

(Continued from page 35)

"When someone's working alone, it's easy to start second-guessing. Did my boss really like that report? Why haven't I had more feedback?" Pape says. "In new hires look for people who feel secure about their job skills and personal lives. The best predictor of future success is often past success." Then, once you hire a remote worker, make sure to keep company news available online, and stay in frequent communication by phone or video-conference.

   ❧ *Does the person have a good sense of humor?* "People with a good sense of humor—who consequently are slow to anger—tend to deal more effectively with the frustrations of the virtual workplace," Pape observes. "They tend to be more productive."

   ❧ *How well does the candidate cope with technology?* "Hire people who have demonstrated that they're not afraid of technology," Pape suggests. "Do they own a PC? How often do they use it? How do they solve a computer problem?" Even the technologically sophisticated will inevitably run into problems, however. The next step? "Back up your folks with a corporate help desk to walk them through the problems they're certainly going to encounter," Pape advises.

17

IDEA

Practice Teachers

At DigitalMoon Learning Studios, a Norwalk, Conn., company that conducts Macintosh training, prospective trainers and salespeople need more than good interviewing skills and glowing references. "We're hiring people for their ability to get up in front of six people they don't know and present material," says CEO David Knise. So before the company makes a final hiring decision, Knise **puts candidates on the hot seat by requiring them to demonstrate their skills**.

Knise asks job candidates to make an hour-long presentation to his seven-member staff on any topic other than computers. "Because we're computer people, we'd focus too much on whether what they say is right or wrong, and not on their ability to teach," he explains. A report on the solar system was given a thumbs-up, as was a presentation on the instruments in an orchestra. Attempts to teach Italian, in-line skating, and math were deemed unsuccessful.

"We see how applicants organize their thoughts, if they've given themselves enough time to cover the material, and if they have overall command of a classroom," says Knise. He also notes how candidates react to disruptive participants and whether they appear to be focusing on him during their talk. "The more confident people don't play to me as much," he says. The success of this auditioning strategy can be seen in the high marks DigitalMoon's trainers generally receive on written evaluations from customers.

Knise's approach focuses on job candidates' presentation skills, but you can also develop auditioning techniques to test other types of skills. For example, Sean McEwen, chairman and CEO of TriTech   *(Continued)*

(Continued from page 37)

Software Systems, a San Diego-based company that produces dispatching systems and software for the public-safety industry, needs to assess the abilities of technical writers before hiring them. But he has never put much stock in writing samples because he knows that candidates will simply supply one or two of their best efforts. So McEwen gives an assignment to prospects who want a job writing manuals at his company. Go home tonight, he tells recruits, and write a manual about hand washing. "It's something so basic; it's something we all know how to do," explains McEwen. "And we're all experts on judging the quality of the manual. I could give it to the person who answers the phones, and she'd have a valid opinion of it."

McEwen must be doing something right. TriTech Software Systems has grown so quickly that it made the 1998 *Inc.* 500 list of fastest-growing privately held U.S. businesses. In 1993, 10 years after its founding, the company had sales of more than $1 million. By 1999, sales were expected to grow to $19 million.

18
IDEA

Tag Teams

Ric Edelman, CEO of Edelman Financial Center, in Fairfax, Va., believes an all-inclusive hiring process helps create a close-knit atmosphere with very low turnover at his company, which had 1998 revenues of $11.6 million. No applicant wins a job in any of the financial planning and investment-management company's six subsidiaries without facing **grueling officewide scrutiny**.

First, potential hires are screened by telephone. Then as many as 10 applicants per job opening are interviewed, usually by employees from the division that has the opening. Finally, the top two or three candidates return for final interviews with teams of two or three Edelman employees. The employees who conduct the interviews receive training in the legal issues that surround job interviews, Edelman notes. "We're very sensitive to those rules," he says.

If any team turns thumbs down, not even Edelman can veto the decision. He says the strategy both reduces turnover and yields "high-quality people, because employees hire in their own image."

19
IDEA

Hiring Blind

Hiring is difficult under most circumstances, but in a virtual corporation that has global operations, bringing on new employees poses special challenges. "The process is that much harder for a virtual corporation, where interviews must be conducted and skills tested remotely," observes Will Pape, cofounder of VeriFone. Here's how Pape addressed those challenges in 1995, when hiring someone to succeed himself as VeriFone's chief information officer. (VeriFone, which makes electronic payment systems, is based in Santa Clara, Calif., and has since been acquired by Hewlett-Packard.)

The key to Pape's hiring strategy? A committee. "I knew I needed the buy-in of both information systems staff and the department's internal customers," he recalls. "I'm generally not a big fan of committees, but when you're trying to draw on a variety of expertise and perspectives, sometimes they're the only way." In this case, the search committee included three people from the information systems department, a manager from another department, and Pape.

Pape believes that **including subordinates in the hiring process** is particularly important in a virtual company like VeriFone. "When you're reporting to someone you scarcely ever see, helping choose that person can instill much-needed comfort and confidence," he notes.

The hiring committee's duties were broad-based—everything from updating the job description to conducting interviews to helping Pape make the final decision. The committee was assisted by 10 of the company's vice-presidents, who agreed to interview the three finalists. Because none of the hiring committee members worked in the same location, the committee used telephone, e-mail, and videoconferencing to communicate. Videoconferencing was particularly helpful in the group's early meetings, Pape recalls, because some of the committee members had never met. "Initially we relegated e-mail, which is more likely to cause misunderstandings than voice or video, to logistics management," he explains. "As we got to know and understand one another better, however, our e-mail increasingly carried more substantive communications."

The committee process was not without pitfalls. "Managing a virtual hiring committee is like moderating a globally dispersed McLaughlin Group," observes Pape. "Each panel member has a viewpoint (often passionately expressed) that has been informed by geography, culture, and work environment. And because most members interact with the candidates and one another remotely, they are likely to emerge from meetings and interviews with very different impressions."

To overcome such differences, Pape asked the committee members to rank the candidates for the job every time the group obtained new information from, say, an interview or a new résumé. Then committee members would share their rankings and the reasons for them. Pape also encouraged the group to brainstorm during conference calls about subjects such as the characteristics important to success on the job. The committee then conducted most of the initial interviews via conference calls, so that each candidate could talk to the whole committee.

"Over the years, I've encountered many people who assumed they'd be good at virtual management but then—after being hired and put to the test—simply weren't," says Pape. "Conducting virtual interviews had become a kind of remote skills testing for VeriFone. If candidates performed well in what is an inherently stressful situation, we *(Continued)*

(Continued from page 41)

were reasonably confident that they were up to the challenge of virtual work."

The committee's work didn't end when the new hire was chosen, either. The next step was helping her assimilate. For new employees, "most really useful knowledge comes from informal conversations with veteran workers and simple observation of how people do things," Pape argues. "The trick to assimilating a virtual employee is to duplicate those informal mentoring, tutoring, and nurturing systems."

Pape's solution? "I asked my committee members to be the new hire's 'buddies,' to help bring her up to speed as quickly as possible," he explains. "And because of their involvement in her hiring and what they felt was their stake in her success, they were very effective. One man spent hours talking with the new director about the subtleties—both operational and personal—of more than 60 online systems, and for three months made sure she was thoroughly briefed before she met the customers for each system."

Pape thinks that other virtual corporations could learn from the hiring method that VeriFone developed. "VeriFone's hiring process returned superb results, improving the caliber of new hires and helping build relationships between new employees and their colleagues and subordinates," he says. "For any company that operates virtually and cares deeply about employing good people, this is by far the best method I've found for bringing outsiders into the fold."

20
IDEA

Executive Temps

Growing entrepreneurial companies often need a certain type of professional skill but aren't ready to add someone long-term to the payroll and company benefits plan. At such times it can make sense to **"rent" the needed talent on a short-term basis, even at the executive level**.

Ask Rick Kearney, the president of Mainline Information Systems, a marketer of computer equipment and support services in Tallahassee, Fla.

"Back in June of 1994 we were doing about $3 million in sales," he recalls, "and aimed to compete with larger companies as they downsized and cut back on support services. However, although our business plan was good and the quality of our technical staffing was very high, we lacked serious financial expertise." Mainline's only financial staffer was Kearney's wife, the company's bookkeeper.

Then a big business break forced a change. "We won a contract to provide Florida school systems with personal computers. It was going to double our sales overnight, but I had to get a line of credit that would pay for the equipment, shipping, and support-staff upgrades."

Kearney thought his company still wasn't ready to commit to hiring a full-time chief financial officer, since CFOs in his region commanded about $120,000 a year plus benefits at that time. Some business owners might have turned to an accounting firm, but Kearney believed Mainline needed expertise beyond the capabilities of certified public accountants. "We needed someone with specialized knowledge about raising capital, as well as about my industry."

After asking for names in his industry, Kearney turned to *(Continued)*

(Continued from page 43)

an Atlanta-based consulting firm that allowed him to "basically, rent a CFO with expertise in both my industry and the capital markets." Kearney contracted for the CFO to visit Mainline for two weeks each month. His mission was to help the company assess its financing needs, prepare financial statements along with a business plan to support the financing pitch, and ultimately, to win financing.

"It was a complete success," says Kearney. "He helped us figure out that we needed $4 million, gathered all the financial information we needed, helped us identify possible financiers, and then prepared us for their questions. With his help we landed a $4-million line of credit, with a 15- to 45-day interest-free grace period, from IBM Credit Corp." The cushion helped Mainline at a time when its receivables took as long as 90 days to collect.

Sixteen months of the rent-a-CFO's half-time assistance cost Mainline about $135,000, less than the cost of a full-time CFO for that period. Plus, Kearney had the advantage of the trial period without committing to a full-time employee. Kearney has no regrets, "because he achieved all his goals and then he left, without causing any drag on our payroll." Kearney subsequently hired a full-time CFO, and Mainline continued to grow. "We now have our own CFO and a chief of operations and comptroller and a CPA in-house," says Kearney, whose *Inc.* 500 company had revenues of $70.7 million in 1997. "Our financial division has certainly grown quite a bit."

"The best training is the kind you provide because people really want a job, really want the opportunity. You tell them what qualifications they need and give them the chance to go for it. Then they'll make sure the training dollars are well spent—assuming you have to spend anything at all."

JACK STACK
president and CEO,
Springfield ReManufacturing Corp.;
author, with Bo Burlingham,
of *The Great Game of Business*
(Doubleday/Currency)

21
IDEA

Bring School to Work

Nancy Sanders Peterson, president and CEO of Peterson Tool, had a problem all too common today. Many of the workers at her Nashville company—which designs and manufactures specialized metal-working cutting tools—were short on math skills. But Peterson couldn't afford to send more than 10% of her 165 employees back to high school. Instead, she **took advantage of a state-funded training program**. At no cost to Peterson, high-school teachers visited the company twice a week to teach math classes between workers' shifts. A few employees even went so far as to take the GED (General Educational Development) high-school equivalency test. Peterson believes the math training really paid off. For example, she says, her company subsequently obtained its ISO 9000 certification.

About 45 states offer some form of training subsidies to businesses, according to a 1999 report by Sacramento-based Steve Duscha Advisories. Criteria for the programs vary by state.

Cross-Training

During a company's frenzied start-up days, staffers often have so many different duties that some entrepreneurial companies forego job descriptions entirely. Later, as companies grow, employees tend to specialize. But some CEOs argue that it's important for employees to remain flexible. The better **everyone knows everyone else's job**, the thinking goes, the better the company runs.

To foster that kind of flexibility, more companies are cross-training—instructing employees in the essential elements of a number of different jobs within the organization, regardless of whether they are likely ever to perform those jobs. Despite the costs of such training, proponents say the benefits are numerous.

One obvious benefit is higher employee morale. GreenPages, a computer reseller in Kittery, Maine, which had 1998 sales of $88 million, puts each new employee through two months of intensive training in all job functions. Customer-support people get sales training, salespeople learn about purchasing and credit services, and so on. That, according to CEO Kurt Bleicken, promotes mutual understanding. "When people are familiar with what the rest of the company is doing," he says, "it breaks down the typical 'us versus them' attitude."

Cross-training also helps companies ensure that:

Every employee can help a customer. At The Chip, a Valencia, Calif., computer technical support and repair company with 1998 revenues of $4 million, everyone is trained in computer repair—including the receptionist. That way, whoever answers the phone is able to address *(Continued)*

(Continued from page 47)

technical problems. According to president Chip Meyer, the company phones can act as a de facto help desk for clients.

❧ *Every employee knows how to sell.* For Nick Nicholson, CEO of a recycling and waste-management company in Columbus, Ohio, with 1998 revenues of $40 million, it was important that each of his employees understand the sales process. All Ecology Group staff members received sales training, including classes on good questioning and listening skills. Once, a member of the accounting staff was on the phone with a client who had a huge over-billing problem. In the process of clarifying the problem, the employee identified an opportunity to extend the Ecology Group's agreement with the client, involving more locations and more business. "I don't think he could have done that if he hadn't had sales training," says Nicholson.

❧ *No employee is indispensable.* Kurt Bleicken of GreenPages, which is a two-time *Inc.* 500 company, also uses cross-training to counteract short- and long-term leaves of absence, such as maternity leaves, among his 125 employees. He has two highly cross-trained individuals whom he calls "GreenPage runners." These employees can fill many positions in the company—purchasing, sales, credit services, or accounting. And they can sub for almost any length of time, covering everything from sick days or vacations to extended sabbaticals. Of course, since the runners are generalists by definition, they're not always as effective as regular employees. But when you're anxious to keep the sales flow even, for instance, "it's better than starting over from square one," Bleicken says.

23
IDEA

No Train, No Gain

Some busy CEOs regard employee training with the same dismay many of us feel about exercise—it's a great idea, and it's essential to our well-being, but who has the time for it? That attitude doesn't wash with Connie Connors, who has a "just do it" attitude. "To maintain our competitive advantage, we have to train," says Connors, president and CEO of a 50-employee public-relations firm, Connors Communications, in New York City. So, through a number of in-house programs, Connors **integrated education into the culture of her company**—which counted 1998 revenues in excess of $6 million. Here are some of the ways she did it.

➤ *TIPs (Tips for Improving Performance).* On-site training sessions are held approximately every two weeks for 15 minutes. The employees who constitute the training committee set up minisessions based on employee feedback. "TIPs have ranged from HTML coding to perfecting your pitch," explains Connors. The firm's employees or outside experts run the TIPs. Because the nonmandatory sessions are short (okay, they really last closer to half an hour) and are held on-site, they're usually well attended. Employees are also encouraged to attend industry or skill-related conferences and seminars.

➤ *Annual company meetings that include training sessions.* One year, Connors used a three-day retreat in the Catskills to explain the company's pricing structure and teach effective schmoozing in a simulated cocktail-party setting.

➤ *The "Connors Bible."* This section of the company's intranet gives employees instant access to information about clients, as *(Continued)*

(Continued from page 49)

well as company philosophy, organizational structure, procedures, and policies.

ε *The buddy system.* For their first two months at the company, new employees have designated buddies who are "close to their levels—definitely not the people they report to," explains Connors. A buddy might, for instance, give a neophyte the skinny on office politics. That's not training per se, but since the company has grown rapidly, Connors thinks it's crucial that new hires become familiar with the intangibles.

ε *Committees.* Like the buddy system, Connors's committee system isn't, strictly speaking, a training program. Still, by encouraging employees to form committees to address issues that concern and interest them, Connors has, in effect, created another method of continuing employee education and development. "Our employees all participate in some committee," she says, but they can choose the one that interests them. The committees cover such subjects as marketing, finance, international dealings, and creativity.

What's the effect of the company's commitment to training? Connie Connors thinks her training programs help her retain employees longer than usual for her industry and result in employees providing better service.

24
IDEA

Acting Out

Want to make your training sessions memorable? Put drama on the menu. Stan Frankenthaler, chef and president of Salamander Restaurant, in Cambridge, Mass., brings an element of theater to his ongoing training sessions. Once a week waitpeople at the restaurant act out scenarios such as medical emergencies and computer breakdowns. "Verbal instructions are often hit-or-miss," says Frankenthaler, who estimates that his restaurant's revenues will reach $2.25 million in 1999. "When the staff is actively involved in training, the lessons are longer-lasting." There's another payoff: Working together to perform the skits fosters camaraderie among the employees.

Mark Leavitt, president of MedicaLogic, in Hillsboro, Ore., uses skits to train both employees and customers. MedicaLogic, which makes electronic medical-records software and had 1998 revenues of $17 million, holds half-day "clinic work-flow simulations." Groups of new employees (or a new client's medical-office staff) take turns playing doctor or patient or receptionist and responding to various crises that have been known to occur in a medical-office setting. Leavitt says customers are better prepared for their first day with the software system "because they've been through it before." Employees, meanwhile, can better design, sell, and service the product once they are more familiar with the operation of a medical clinic.

While **role-playing, simulations, and skits** are useful for training all types of employees, they can be particularly critical if your employees aren't academically inclined. At Cooperative Home Care Associates, a home-health-care company in the Bronx, N.Y., the sole product is the *(Continued)*

(Continued from page 51)

service its home health aides provide. To president Rick Surpin, that means the company, which took in $7 million in 1998 revenues, should invest as much in training as it can afford. But, most of the entry-level employees at Cooperative Home Care have only an eighth-grade reading level or less, according to Surpin. Because so many don't have a strong education, it's important to deliver the training in a way that won't alienate them. "Most of them hated school," he says. "The worst kind of training for the folks we work with is to sit them in classrooms and make them listen to lectures."

While some subjects in its pre-employment training must be covered in lectures, Cooperative Home Care tries to address many topics through hands-on demonstrations. And, the company goes farther toward making entry-level employees feel comfortable. By law, Cooperative Home Care's home-health-care courses must have a nurse in the classroom at all times. But, the company also adds assistants who themselves have worked as home health aides. That way, new employees have instructors to whom they can relate.

25
IDEA

Show and Tell

Managers at FGM, a Herndon, Va., company with 1998 revenues of $15 million, found a way to improve employees' presentation skills while fostering workplace camaraderie. This 1997 *Inc.* 500 company, which develops computer software and integrates computer systems, holds weekly **brown-bag lunch seminars where employees hone their speaking skills** in front of volunteer audiences of 10 to 30 of their colleagues. The speakers, who are also volunteers, receive T-shirts and enter FGM's annual speakers' contest.

"It's great, especially for young engineers who don't have experience getting up in front of customers. That was definitely in the back of my mind," says CEO Scott Gessay. On occasion, customers are also invited to the Thursday seminars—one client sat in on a session about Java technology, for example.

What started a number of years ago as a purely technical exchange has expanded into a platform for a variety of business and personal interests. Seminar topics range from advances in 3-D animation to Guitar 101. "People in different parts of the company get to share their knowledge," says Gessay, who, along with 14 others, attended the guitar seminar led by a blues-playing staffer.

26
IDEA

Good Grooming

Michael Horgan, president and CEO of JPL Productions in Harrisburg, Pa., wanted to prevent newly promoted managers from "bombing because they are given a totally different group of tasks to perform." So, he devised a clever and inexpensive program at his media-production company to **test and improve employees' management skills before they become managers**.

At JPL, employees are required to manage student interns for three-month periods before being promoted to management jobs. At the end of the period, each employee mentor evaluates the intern, and interns review their managers. Having employees try their hand at supervising interns "allows us to evaluate their management skills for the future," Horgan says. As an added benefit, Horgan observes, employees who have managed interns tend to respect their own managers more. Clearly, the program works: Six out of the seven managers at JPL, which had sales of $2.8 million in 1998, have been promoted from within.

Leading Lessons

How do we go about changing ourselves so we can have a fully empowered, fully integrated, and committed workforce, so we all function as a team rather than 'us versus them'?" That was the question Bill Budinger, chairman and founder of Rodel, was asking himself in the early 1990s. At the time, Rodel, which is based in Newark, Del., was increasingly challenged by Japanese competitors whose corporate cultures emphasized teamwork. So, as part of its response to the new competition, Rodel developed an **in-house leadership-training program**.

All 350 employees at the company, which manufactures polishing pads and slurries used to process silicon wafers and microchips, were invited to apply to take part in the year-long program, dubbed Leadership Intensive Training. Applicants were asked to respond in writing to questions such as, "The key to leadership is being a passionate advocate for something that forwards our mission. What are you a passionate advocate for?" and "What eventual responsibility or position do you see for yourself at Rodel?"

About half the employees who applied were accepted—they ranged from executives to factory workers. Each person was asked to set individual goals for the year, and the group was given a 12-month class project. The assignment: to reduce production-waste material at the company from 18% to 10%. Two top executives in the class exempted themselves from that project, so that the rest of the class would be forced to work together to tackle the problem, rather than relying on executive fiat.

"With no lines of authority to lean on, they were forced to have leadership emerge," says Lloyd Fickett, a Phoenix-based manage-   *(Continued)*

(Continued from page 55)

ment consultant who works as a part-time executive at Rodel and who taught the class. "Natural leaders tried to dominate the situation, but without the power that comes from position, they had to exert influence through persuasion. People learned that leadership isn't always easy or convenient, and that sometimes it means being a good follower."

The group eventually split into five teams to handle different facets of the project, and group members needed to enlist the support of employees throughout the company to accomplish their goal. As a result, the group learned to work together and across department lines. Along the way, the class also read books on leadership and discussed examples of it, so that the course included theory and practice.

At the end of the year, the class had not fully accomplished its waste-reduction goal, but it had managed to save the company $200,000. Since the program cost about $40,000, including Fickett's time, the company was pleased with the results, Budinger says.

In fact, Rodel executives liked it well enough to repeat the program twice. Budinger reports that the leadership program, along with other initiatives such as open-book management, helped the company's sales grow 30% to 50% annually since 1993, to almost $250 million in 1998.

Meaningful Mentoring

Michael Parks, CEO of the Revere Group, a Chicago-based technology consulting firm with projected 1999 revenues of $55 million, knows it's hard to grow a company if your employees don't grow, too. So, the Revere Group has had a **"career-pathing" program** almost since Parks started the business in 1992.

At the beginning of the year, the company assigns a mentor to each Revere Group employee. After a bit of experimentation, Parks learned that having a manager mentor the employees who report to him or her didn't work. "It's a natural conflict," he says. "If I'm your manager and you want to make a change, how can you tell me that you really don't want to work in my area?" So, he selects mentors not by titles or tenure but by their people skills and knowledge of both the company and the industry.

The employee and the mentor sit down and develop an individual growth plan that details how the employee will spend the two weeks of annual training that Revere Group requires, as well as what progress he or she needs to make to obtain a promotion or change jobs. Employees receive quarterly updates on their progress and have periodic check-ins with their mentors. Besides developing a more effective workforce, Parks reports that the program has boosted employee retention.

29
IDEA

Company Campus

Your business doesn't have to be big to have an in-house "university" training program. And, having one doesn't mean you have an institutional ego bent on molding men and women into company clones. An increasing number of growing businesses are starting universities—**ongoing skill-enhancement programs** that draw on internal and external resources to train new employees and keep veteran ones current with a rapidly changing business environment.

"Training isn't just a nice thing to do anymore," says Laurie Bassi, vice-president of research at the American Society for Training and Development, in Alexandria, Va. "Companies are now thinking of training as a strategic imperative." Companies with in-house universities report several benefits, including:

❧ *Improved recruitment.* Edward Beaumont, CEO of CoreTech Consulting Group, in King of Prussia, Pa., says that his technology consulting company, which reported 1998 revenues of $42 million, uses training as a key recruitment lure. "We needed a robust training and education facility to be competitive," he says. So, he started CoreTech University, offering short training sessions to help employees hone both technical and interpersonal skills, such as quality management and team building. The program, which draws on employee instructors as well as professors at Pennsylvania State University and Drexel University, was not so much a differentiator for the company as it was a requirement, says Beaumont. "We're finding that compensation is less of an issue for employees and that growth and career development are more important," he says.

If CoreTech University sounds like an extravagance, consider this: The company used the curriculum to create CoreTech Institute, which has been sold as a separate for-profit training organization (renamed CTI) that offers courses to the public, particularly to chief information officers and information technology managers. (Core Tech still offers in-house training, but not through CTI.)

❧ *Employee growth.* Bob Kirkpatrick, CoreTech's chief people officer (yes, that's his real title), estimates that the company spends approximately $4,500 annually to train each of its approximately 350 employees. However, he says, it's money well spent. Employees can use CoreTech's training to become officially certified, for example, as a project manager or a Microsoft Certified Systems Engineer. Every employee is required to take (primarily on company time) technical and "soft skills" training courses that are linked to the company's overall mission. For instance, a course in project management is tied directly to the company's quality goals.

❧ *Reduced turnover.* Douglas Palley measures the success of his "university" through the significant drop in turnover at Unitel, his call-center company in McLean, Va. Since he started Unitel University a few years ago, average monthly turnover has dropped from 12% to 6%, a dramatic change for a company staffed primarily by low-wage employees. "Unemployment in our area was 1.5%. We were looking for ways to improve retention and morale and to give people a career track," says Palley, whose company reported $12.2 million in 1997 sales.

As part of Unitel U., entry-level employees can take courses such as computer training and customer service through a variety of self-directed study programs or they can take courses at a local university. Palley spent $150,000 on the program the first year. Judging by the decrease in turnover, he concludes that Unitel U. is "very close to the break-even point."   *(Continued)*

(Continued from page 59)

❧ *Better employee advancement.* After 90 days at Unitel, newcomers are eligible to become "freshmen" at the university and can take several more hours of classes beyond their initial orientation courses. If they pass, they receive a raise of up to 8% of their pay. Then, every 90 days, employees can take more in-depth courses in telephone sales, customer service, and computer skills. When they successfully complete each level, they earn another raise of up to 8%. Criteria for passing are rigorous, says Palley, and "if they're late twice in a 90-day period, they have to start that level over again." The program isn't mandatory, but employees know that training is the quickest path to increased pay and responsibility. "It's been an outstanding recruiting tool," says Palley.

❧ *A wider talent pool.* Jane Callanan, vice-president of human resources at i-Cube, a Cambridge, Mass., information-technology consulting services company that reported revenues of $42 million in 1998, credits her company's internal university with easing the heavy burden of recruiting 155 people in two years. "The hiring landscape was pitiful," she recalls. "We wanted to tap into college recruiting, to hire people who were very bright but didn't have several years of work experience." A five-week, 9-to-5 program, called i-Altitude, staffed primarily by senior managers, allowed the company to hire workers with little experience, then give them the technical training they needed to serve clients. "It really opened the labor market for us," says Callanan. "We can hire physics majors with a 3.8 grade point average but no computer-science training. After five weeks, they're ready for a project. You can't do that without a good educational program."

Field Trips

When Lisa Lorimer's company, Vermont Bread, in Brattleboro, Vt., went through a growth spurt several years ago, sales doubled in just two years. To help prepare her staff to meet the challenges of fast growth, Lorimer began arranging for **employees to meet their counterparts at bigger companies**. "We get about a dozen people into a van and travel to several companies," says Lorimer, whose company had 1998 sales of $10 million. "We talk to the people on the floor rather than to the CEO. I sit back and let my employees do the talking."

Lorimer got the idea for the field trips when she noticed how valuable it was to network with her own peers at other companies. She decided she wanted her employees to have that opportunity, too. Most companies, Lorimer reports, were more than willing to "let us in behind their facade," she says. "It's just a wonderful time to connect with other businesses."

In fact, Lorimer liked the results of the visits so well that she organized another round of trips when her company was planning a big automation project. This time, she and some of her staff visited other automated bakeries, mostly companies serving different market niches or serving local markets different from those her own company targeted. "We wanted to see what other people had done," she says. "We've come back with some great ideas."

31
IDEA

New Boss on the Block

Many entrepreneurs have a problem bringing outside managers into their companies. Kevin Owens, CEO of Select Design, a producer of custom corporate sportswear and related items in Burlington, Vt., avoided pitfalls by working out **a careful transition to integrate the new hire**, a sales manager, into the business.

Owens recruited his sales manager just after passing $1 million in revenues. "We hired him a little bit before we had to, because we anticipated the training effort. Although this person had 10 years of industry experience, my partner and I needed to spend a lot of time with him on the company's image and story." For the first year, for instance, Owens scheduled time to talk about such things before and after the sales chief made a presentation. And when he first came on board, Owens handed over some—but not all—of the company's key accounts to him.

The arrangements put some healthy pressure on the manager to prove he could bring in new customers (he did), and it has allowed Owens to keep a hand in sales. Four and a half years after his arrival, the sales manager has made a crucial contribution to bringing the company to the next level. In 1998, Select Design had about 50 employees, and sales had reached $5 million.

32
IDEA

The Making of the President

In 1997, Dennis Brozak passed the day-to-day operation of his company, Design Basics, which had revenues of $4 million, to a new president, Linda Reimer. Where did he find her? At the copy machine. In retrospect, it's clear that Reimer had management potential, but the long-term systematic training that Brozak provided also contributed to Reimer's advancement.

Back in 1991, Reimer was a longtime preschool director who wanted a part-time summer job. She took a low-level job photocopying blueprints for Design Basics, an Omaha-based company that sells blueprints for homes via catalog. She did that job so well that Brozak hired her full-time in 1994.

Over the next two years, Brozak gave Reimer various **assignments that tested the potential executive's leadership capabilities**. First, he made her a human-resources director and asked her to switch the department's focus from advocating employees' rights to developing their professional growth. She succeeded. Brozak began challenging her more and more. "I wanted to find out a lot about her," he says. "Can she manage and motivate people? Can she delegate accurately and appropriately? And she had to be able to fire people when necessary. She has a big heart, but she passed that test, too."

Then, to see if she understood the market and the industry, Brozak put Reimer in charge of one product, a catalog. The catalog's home designs sold well. Brozak then evaluated her financial acumen by making her an operations director, and he watched how well she used the company's money. Again, he says, she did well. So Brozak gave her *(Continued)*

(Continued from page 63)

control over all the company's publishing. Once more, she produced a hit.

Finally, Brozak tested Reimer, by then a vice-president, with new product development. He figured that assignment would show whether she was a big-picture thinker. Reimer identified a new niche that has become a major profit center for the company. "She changed the direction of our sales," Brozak says.

By 1996, after 13 years at the company's helm, Brozak wanted more free time. He began passing day-to-day operations to Reimer, giving her new responsibilities gradually to make sure she was ready to be promoted. In April 1997, Reimer officially became president. CEO Brozak says revenues are expected to grow to $5.2 million in 1999.

What's the secret to identifying hidden leaders in your company? Here are some traits that Brozak looked for, and found, in Reimer.

- *Curiosity.* "I couldn't learn fast enough about business," Reimer says of her early days at Design Basics. "I was like a sponge."

- *An affinity for finance.* Finance is a broader subject than accounting, notes Brozak. There's a difference between recording the history of money and keeping it in constant motion.

- *Shared values.* It's important to Brozak that Reimer relate to his core values: that all work is honorable and that everyone be paid a fair wage.

- *Passion for the business.* Reimer's mother designed homes, and her father built them. Their love for building has been passed down.

- *The ability to work well with the founder.* "You need someone who can deal with the owner who grew the company from scratch—and who's still around," says Brozak.

IV

"The number one thing employees want more of is not money. Rather, more than anything else employees want to feel that their work is making a contribution toward the good of the company, and they want to have time off with their families."

DAVID DeCAPUA
vice-president and partner,
Dawson Personnel Systems
Columbus, Ohio

33
IDEA

Measure of Success

Wouldn't it be great if you could quantify each employee's performance before handing out money? Some entrepreneurs try to get a handle on how much individuals are contributing to the business—as well as encouraging increased employee performance—by developing **incentive pay plans that vary by job category or department**.

Take the case of Career TEAM, a fast-growing Hamden, Conn., company that reported $4 million in 1998 revenues. CEO Christopher Kuselias sets quantitative goals for every member of his 25-person staff. But at Career TEAM, whose business consists of placing welfare recipients in jobs and then monitoring their progress in those jobs, each employee's goals include individual, departmental, and companywide measures. That mix, Kuselias says, helps mitigate the "me-first" urge that can accompany individual incentives; in that way, he hopes to encourage employees to add value to the entire company.

Kuselias says that Career TEAM receives funding based on its success at reaching three benchmarks: the number of welfare recipients who complete the company's training programs, the number who are placed in jobs, and the number who stay on those jobs six months. "We only get paid when someone is successful," he says. So, Kuselias uses those three benchmarks in his incentive pay plan, too. Typically, he says, about 70% of an employee's incentive pay will be based on the benchmark he or she influences the most. For example, the incentive pay of an employee involved in teaching the training program will be based primarily on the training-completion statistics. To encourage interdepartmental cooperation, Kuselias bases the remainder of the employee's incentive pay package on the other two benchmark measurements.

However, compensation systems of this type rarely remain static. At In-Seitz, a 40-employee communication agency with offices in Rochester, N.Y., and Atlanta, CEO Charles Engler has been adjusting his incentive compensation system periodically since its inception in 1989. At that time, Engler switched from an overtime pay system to profit sharing, to stop the company from losing money. "We had to change to a system that rewarded people for making money, so the company would make money," Engler recalls.

Engler has refined his system so that different departments have different performance measurements. For example, Engler measures the time it takes his computer-support staff to respond to requests for repairs—as well as overall system downtime. Meanwhile, production people are evaluated on a combination of their own productivity, the profitability of the projects they work on, and customer-satisfaction measurements. Engler's overall aim? To tie employees' compensation as closely as possible to what makes the company profitable.

"If you refine the desire to know how well people are performing, you are really trying to measure the amount of money they generate for the company. It is desirable to know this so that you can reward and encourage people to do more of what makes the company money," he notes. "Thus the company should make even more money."

One caveat: any type of incentive-pay plan has perils as well as potential. Such plans are more likely to succeed if:

&. *They're explained properly.* Jerry McAdams, a national practice leader of Watson Wyatt Worldwide and the author of *The Reward Plan Advantage*, suggests that you focus as much on explaining and *(Continued)*

(Continued from page 67)

implementing your incentive-pay system as you do on designing it. "Research has shown that the more you communicate with and engage employees, the less money you'll need to have in terms of payout," he says. "A poorly designed plan well implemented will always do better than a well-designed plan poorly implemented."

They're farsighted. "Watch out what you reinforce," McAdams notes. "You're likely to get it." Designed unwisely, incentive systems can encourage employees to be penny-wise and pound-foolish. For example, if an employee's goals focus only on cutting costs, he or she may ignore opportunities that build value, yet cost money.

They have targets that change regularly. Every incentive plan, McAdams says, should be reexamined every year as part of your business strategy. "The longer you keep it the same, the more it becomes perceived as an entitlement," he says. However, changes while an incentive program is in progress undermine trust in the system. As a result, it makes sense to let employees know from the start when goals will change.

They're clear, not confusing. Measure whatever business measures you want, suggests McAdams, but base the incentive pay employees receive on no more than three to four numbers. That's all most people can focus on effectively.

34
IDEA

Custom Packaging for Paychecks

Stock options. Lucrative bonuses. High starting salaries. Flex time. What kind of compensation matters most to experienced managers? There's no universal answer. And there's no universal standard for executive compensation packages any more. Today, each high-level candidate is looking for a slightly different type of opportunity. Understand that, and you'll understand why there's never been a better time to attract senior talent. Scores of recruiters, company owners, human resource directors, and recruits agree. For the right opportunity, a lot of heavy hitters are willing to make considerable compensation tradeoffs—even when it comes to base salary. In general, **bonus plans with escalating payouts** (usually tied to such metrics as growth in sales, profits, cash flow, or a company's valuation) are increasingly popular forms of executive compensation.

"I want to make a decent salary, but I'm not motivated by money and never have been," says Tom King, a banking veteran who took a sizable pay cut to join a much smaller company. In April 1999 King became the new president of Reliant Professionals, a staffing agency in San Diego. "I got typecast as a turnaround specialist, and I was tired of doing turnarounds," King explains. "I toyed with retiring. Now I'm excited about having a new challenge."

As president of Reliant Professionals, King does not have a grandiose compensation package, but there is potential for him to be richly rewarded. Once the company is profitable, and as long as quarterly targets are reached, King will receive a fixed percentage of pretax profits right off the top. King also negotiated his own version of a severance   *(Continued)*

(Continued from page 69)

payment, or what some would call a "change-in-control" bonus. Should owner Dana Dodds sell Reliant Professionals before three years are up, King will receive a lump sum to make up for any compensation he lost when he took a pay cut to join the staffing agency.

Dodds, who also owns Reliant General Insurance Services, is thrilled that he was able to attract a strong candidate like King. Not long ago, Dodds would have agonized over whether he could afford such an experienced executive. He couldn't offer any real equity or even perks like a company car. "How am I going to raid these large companies for the talent I need?" Dodds used to wonder. But hiring the right top people turned out to be "a piece of cake," Dodds says. He signed on three other top managers besides King, two of them from rivals 10 times the size of his insurance company.

Recruiters say it's not unusual to see cash incentives equivalent to 30%—or even 100%—of salary, typically earned over a period of one to three years. A well-designed executive bonus plan takes the sting out of the lower starting salaries that small, young companies often offer—or the edge off risky stock options. In fact, Dodds has found that a bonus plan can replace the equity piece of a compensation plan. In recent years, the plan he created for the senior team at Reliant General Insurance has paid out as much as 500% of salary.

"People's eyes really open when I show them that," says Dodds.

35
IDEA

Raise the Bar Gradually

L ike many management ideas, John Westrum's bonus plan had its origins in a problem. In the mid-1990s, the home-building company was growing like mad. From 1991 to 1994, Westrum Development's revenues skyrocketed 700%, to $28 million.

But, John Westrum became alarmed when he realized that the demands of dramatic growth were overshadowing the four principles that his company was founded on: quality construction, customer satisfaction, on-time delivery, and on-budget performance. "Customers were unhappy, contractors were screaming at us, and our management of invoices and payments broke down," recalls Westrum.

So, Westrum took his 30 employees on a retreat and enlisted their help in developing measurable goals that would address those four original principles. The result was an 11-point plan that included guidelines addressing the length of construction time, the quality of the construction job as measured by a lengthy checklist, customers' willingness to recommend Westrum to their friends, and so on. As an incentive to employees, Westrum set up a companywide **quarterly bonus pool linked to a series of goals**. The bonus plan at Westrum Development, which is located in Fort Washington, Pa., currently helps employees focus on improving the company.

"For each point, we set intermediate and ultimate goals," says Westrum. "If you set unrealistic goals in the beginning, people will be discouraged." Employees agreed that when intermediate goals had been achieved, Westrum would pay into the bonus pool and then raise the bar to the next goal. For instance, after employees had been rewarded for *(Continued)*

(Continued from page 71)

a 19-day reduction in construction time during two consecutive quarters, the ultimate goal (a 26-day reduction) kicked in. "In the beginning, it was a little bit demoralizing, because we weren't doing as well as we thought we would," says Westrum. In 1994, the plan's first year, only 20% of the pool was paid out.

But Westrum persisted, formatting the company's performance on Excel spreadsheets and graphing the results over the previous four quarters, then posting them. "Employees started focusing not so much on the dollars but on the results," says Westrum. "Anytime we weren't meeting an objective, people would rally behind the person who needed help. After about a year and a half, the effect was phenomenal."

By 1998, Westrum says that his company, which reports $40 million in sales and employs between 45 and 50 people, has met all of its original ultimate goals. To keep the program interesting, Westrum finds that he has to raise and change the goals periodically to match the company's improved performance. He tries to keep the goals challenging enough so that the company, at any given time, is paying out 40% to 70% of the pool.

Bonuses for 1998 were expected to range from $500 to $20,000, depending on seniority, level of experience, and other more subjective criteria, says Westrum. He reports that net margins are up, 94% of customers said they would recommend Westrum to a friend (up from 50% in 1994), and quality inspections of finished homes routinely yield scores of more than 95% (compared with percentages in the low 80s in 1994).

36
IDEA

The End of the Annual Raise?

J ohn Davis, CEO of Air Systems, in San Jose, Calif., now a part of the publicly traded company Group Mac, has successfully reduced a large chunk of his fixed overhead: the annual raise for administrative employees. Nearly all of the approximately 140 employees who work in the office at this air-conditioning and heating contracting company forego the security of a fixed annual raise. In exchange, they get the opportunity to earn much more through bonus programs tied to the company's financial performance.

Davis started his incentive plan after the company experienced a near-fatal downturn—a $600,000 loss in 1990 caused painful layoffs. As the company recovered, Davis wanted to grow without increasing fixed overhead. Instead of annual raises for administrative employees (union workers aren't included), he set up **two bonus pools linked to monthly and quarterly profitability**. The first, which he calls a profit-incentive plan, or PIP, kicks in each month that the company makes its profit projection. The PIP payouts are designed to be the incentive-compensation equivalent of a raise. Davis says the payouts average about 5% to 6% of eligible employees' monthly salary, and each year an employee is entitled to have the percentage increase. The second pool adds quarterly bonus checks that, according to Davis, are worth far more than even a stellar raise if the company makes its profit goals for the quarter. So far, so good: In 1998, Air Systems revenues reached $111 million.

Davis's system has required some tweaking. Under the PIP plan, for example, the longer an employee has been with the company, the higher the portion of the employee's compensation that is not *(Continued)*

(Continued from page 73)

guaranteed. So, every three years, employees can question their base salary using industry benchmarks and opt to add half their monthly PIP profit sharing to their fixed income.

Davis calls his compensation plan "the biggest asset we have for employee retention," and he's determined to see it implemented in the rest of Group Mac. He admits that the company's low base salaries create recruiting challenges. "But, we've got enough history now to show job candidates," he says, adding that those who join the fast-growing company tend to be more willing to take risks.

Davis isn't the only entrepreneur to advocate the concept of moderate base salaries plus an ample bonus plan as a means of rewarding employees while containing fixed costs. In *The Great Game of Business* (Doubleday/ Currency, 1994), the book he co-authored with Bo Burlingham, Jack Stack, well-known CEO of Springfield ReManufacturing Corp., argues that such compensation systems help companies maintain a resourceful mentality. That's because employees share in the company's profits when it does well— but in a way that won't increase fixed costs and thereby impede the company's future ability to compete. "It's like getting a raise, maybe even a very substantial raise, over and above your regular salary, but in a way that doesn't jeopardize your future employment," Stack writes.

A Dip in the Pool

If your workforce understands your business goals, you're more likely to achieve them. And if you give employees an easy way to track how well the business is achieving its goals, they'll be motivated to earn a share in the results. That's why increasing numbers of entrepreneurial companies are using some type of **periodic bonuses tied to a company scoreboard**—whether it's posted in the hallway or electronically on the company intranet.

At Elements IV Interiors—a Dayton, Ohio, office-furniture dealer that had 1998 revenues of $7.2 million—the scoreboard is a simple cartoon that hangs in the employee break room. The cartoon shows a flamingo climbing a ladder to a diving board over an aboveground pool. Every month, support-services manager Heather Patrick tapes the "water level" onto a scale on the side of the pool. That's the company's year-to-date net profit. Employees are learning that the profit level determines how much is available in another important pool—their own bonus pool.

Bruce LaVielle and Kim Duncan, the owners of Elements IV, knew they couldn't pursue net profits without keeping a watchful eye on another number—shipments of Haworth Furniture, the company's primary product line. If Haworth sales ever tank, their company risks losing its valuable franchise. So, the ladder to the diving board is also a scale representing Haworth Furniture sales. Every month, Patrick moves the flamingo up the ladder; the flamingo's foot marks the progress. If the flamingo reaches the top of the ladder and dives into a full pool, then Elements IV has met both of its key goals, and employees get a quarterly bonus.

38
IDEA

A Greener Landscape

Employees who excel at their jobs often get promoted to jobs for which they're less well suited. Their performance drops, they're not happy, and the company suffers. So, how do you **motivate and compensate employees you can't—or shouldn't—promote**? "I had always assumed people wanted to move up the ladder," says Tom Lied, CEO of Lied's Landscape Design and Development, in Sussex, Wis. He discovered this isn't always true after he talked an exceptional worker into accepting a managerial promotion. The employee quit three weeks later because he didn't like bossing others around.

Now Lied's company, which had revenues of $13 million in 1998, rewards valuable employees in other ways. By creating multitiered job categories, Lied has enabled employees to increase their salaries by adding responsibilities, such as teaching others, without changing their basic jobs. He also removed salary caps on jobs, so workers wouldn't hit a wage ceiling. And the staff is compensated for other contributions, such as devising more efficient ways to do work. "It's equally as important to do a job faster and more efficiently as it is to take on a management role," says Lied.

Buying Time

Sometimes a small company can't offer a promising job candidate the salary he or she wants. One solution: Offer a lower salary but throw in the prospect of **a salary review that will take place sooner** than the typical 12-month interval. For example, Pat Thompson of Clarke/Thompson Advertising & Design, a New York City agency with $1.5 million in sales, may offer equity in the future, but for now, she makes up for below-market starting salaries by granting new employees a six-month salary review. For example, in 1999, a Web developer who serves as the agency's director of new media was slated to receive a nice raise at his six-month review.

Some recruiters and company owners say that if you can get to within 10% to 20% of the going rate for salary, or of what a candidate asks for, someone who really wants the job is likely to look forward to getting rewarded for good performance in the foreseeable future. Then you've got room to maneuver until your company grows enough to support a higher payroll and until a new hire proves his or her worth.

REAL
WORLD

"People want things. They want big bonuses. They want expensive fringe benefits. My position is, 'Fine, you can have it, but can you fund it?' A lot of times they can't fund it, and they don't want to take the time to learn how. They want it first—they'll worry about paying for it later. That type of thinking destroys companies."

JACK STACK
president and CEO,
Springfield ReManufacturing Corp.;
author, with Bo Burlingham,
of *The Great Game of Business*
(Doubleday/Currency)

40

IDEA

Grub Stakes

At Jack Hartnett's company, managers have an equity stake in the operations they run. "You've got to give them a piece of the action. That gives them their drive and their desire to hang in and do it well," he says. Hartnett is president of D.L. Rogers, in Bedford, Tex., a company whose primary business is ownership of 59 franchises of Sonic, a drive-in restaurant chain. At those Sonic eateries—which accounted for more than $50 million in 1998 revenues—**in exchange for a percentage of profits, a manager must purchase an equity stake**. For a 25% stake in the restaurant he or she runs, the manager receives 25% of the store's monthly net profits, along with a $1,200 monthly salary.

Managers who have been with D.L. Rogers for more than 18 months also qualify for a bonus of 15% of the net profits of the store they manage—as long as the managers meet several guidelines, such as staying within certain food, labor, and paper costs. And three-year veterans are eligible to buy an additional 1% stake in a new Sonic outlet for about $1,750, as long as they meet certain goals.

To avoid valuation disputes when they leave, Hartnett's managers agree to buy into—and get out of—their investment in each existing store at a price based on the store owner's equity—a figure taken straight from the business's balance sheet. (For a new store, the manager's investment is 25% of that store's initial capitalization.) "They buy in and buy out at equity," Hartnett says. "It's real simple."

Hartnett believes that sharing the profits pays off. In 1998, D.L. Rogers' per-store revenues were nearly 18% higher than the chain's *(Continued)*

(Continued from page 79)

average, while profits were 25% above the norm. In an industry known for high turnover, Hartnett's managers stay about nine years, compared with an industry average of less than two. "Some franchisees in Sonic say to me, 'Jack, I can't believe you sell 25% of your stores to your managers,'" Hartnett says. "I think to myself, 'You'd do a helluva lot better if you did, too.'"

Hartnett is not the first to develop that type of compensation strategy. The founders of Outback Steakhouse faced two big challenges when they started that restaurant company in 1987. They needed start-up cash, and they wanted to create equity opportunities for the restaurant chain's general managers. They nailed both with one solution, similar to Hartnett's. They asked the managers to invest in the company in return for a share of the cash flow that their restaurants generated. That compensation system helped the Tampa-based company grow so that revenues reached more than $1.35 billion in 1998.

A version of this compensation strategy is almost 100 years old. In 1902, a young man opened a dry goods and clothing store in Kemmerer, Wyo., in partnership with two of his former employers. Later, that same fellow jump-started the growth of his retail chain by offering one-third of the stock in each new store to its manager. The result? James Cash Penney's company, incorporated in Utah in 1913, became one of America's retail giants: the J.C. Penney Co.

41
IDEA

Know Your Options

Why give stock options rather than stock? Federal Document Clearing House (FDCH), an electronic publisher of news and information, found out by trial and error. The privately held company, which has more than $1 million in sales and offices in Washington, D.C., and Boston, used to give key employees nonvoting stock periodically. But, the arrangement placed a potential tax burden on employees.

"Since our company is growing rapidly, our stock has also become more valuable," managing director Jim Ellis explains. "That meant we were saddling our employees with a tax liability each time we made them a gift." Under the **strategically designed stock-option plan** the company implemented in 1997, taxes become an issue only when employees exercise the options. Plus, the option plan includes rules regarding employee departures and a three-year vesting schedule to discourage turnover.

While there are different types of stock-option plans, they all give participating employees the right to buy stock in the company within a certain time frame at a specified price. In privately held companies, stock-option plans are most often used when a company expects to go public someday or to be acquired, notes Jim Scannella, a principal in Arthur Andersen's human-capital-services group.

If you do install an option plan, educating your employees is key, as entrepreneur Doug Mellinger discovered. "They just didn't understand." That's how Mellinger, founder and former CEO of PRT Group, a financial services software developer that had 1998 sales of $85.6 million, describes his employees' initial reaction to the stock-option program   *(Continued)*

(Continued from page 81)

in the then-private company. During a business trip with an employee of the New York City-based firm, the employee told Mellinger that options in the company "weren't worth very much" because their purchase ("strike") price was so high—$56 a share. The employee felt he could find countless stocks at lower prices and hence could buy many more shares in those other companies.

Mellinger was stunned. Knowing that PRT had a mere 1.2 million shares outstanding, he tried to explain the difference between price and value. PRT was a company full of paper millionaires who hadn't even bothered to read the documents outlining the option program. "I realized this was a very pervasive problem," Mellinger recalls. "We found that we had very senior executives who had no idea how the program worked." And, Mellinger has discovered PRT's situation was fairly common: "Most of the companies I've met have had the same problems I've had," he says. Before taking PRT public, Mellinger instituted an education program to explain to employees how the stock was valued and how stock options work.

Avoid Being Stuck by Stock

Francesco Pompei, president of Exergen, in Watertown, Mass., thought he was just dismissing a worker when he fired an employee who had been granted company stock. However, the employee's lawyer claimed in court that his client was no ordinary employee. Instead, the lawyer argued, he was a minority shareholder whose fiduciary rights had been violated by the firing. The ensuing court battle lasted eight years. "I hadn't the foggiest idea it would end up this way," Pompei says today of the long, costly legal dispute.

Pompei was fairly lucky. Even though two lower courts had decided in favor of the employee, the Massachusetts Supreme Judicial Court ultimately sided with the employer. In the meantime, Exergen had bought back the employee's stock.

In several other cases, the owners of closely held companies have not done so well after dismissing employees who owned stock. "It could go either way in court," explains lawyer Kevin Scott, a partner with Fox, Rothschild, O'Brien & Frankel, in Philadelphia. "The more lawyers can dress the client up as an oppressed minority shareholder, the better are the plaintiff's chances of prevailing."

Is your company at risk? The most likely target for this type of lawsuit is a closely held company that has granted stock selectively to a small number of key employees. Although sharing equity can be a great way for small, growing companies to recruit and keep talented workers, too many business owners grant stock blindly, without **writing sound shareholder agreements**. Remember, if you grant equity selectively to an individual employee, your relationship changes forever. In particular, as *(Continued)*

(Continued from page 83)

Pompei found, you may encounter problems if you try to fire a minority shareholder. "The employee will argue in court, 'the company didn't fire me for cause but as an excuse to freeze me out of my investment,' " says Scott.

If you do decide to give company stock to employees, notes Scott, many disputes can be avoided simply by putting both parties' expectations in writing, up front. Here are five points that he thinks should be included in the shareholder agreements with your employees.

   State that the employee's status is unaffected by the grant, i.e., that an at-will employee who owns stock remains an at-will employee.

   Give yourself the right to buy back the stock if the employee is fired, quits, becomes permanently disabled, goes bankrupt, or dies.

   Give your company first right of refusal if the employee wants to sell or transfer stock.

   Include a noncompete agreement. After all, shareholding employees have access to inside information.

   Recommend that employees have their own lawyers review the agreement. Otherwise, an employee might say later, "You put something in front of me that I signed. I was relying on the company's attorney."

Phantom of the Operation

Johan Lucey faced a challenge that's a perennial quandary among owners of family businesses and other closely held companies: How to compensate fairly and motivate essential nonfamily managers without granting them equity. "I have one key employee who brings a lot of value to the company," says Lucey, president of Wakefield Distribution Systems, a warehousing, transportation, and moving company based in Danvers, Mass. "I wanted to give her a long-term incentive to stay with us."

Lucey's solution was a **"mirror" or "phantom" stock plan** that his lawyer helped him devise and which was implemented in 1994. This compensation tool is designed to motivate and retain key employees without sharing ownership in the company. Such plans can yield some of the same payoffs as equity grants or stock options. Using phantom stock "it's possible to pass on the same financial reward to executives or others without incurring any of the risks or complications that might accompany the sharing of equity," notes Jim Scannella, a principal in Arthur Andersen's human-capital-services group.

Here's how phantom-stock plans work: You give your executive 1,000 shares of so-called phantom stock at, say, $10 a share. The phantom stock is not actual equity but is tied to the value of your company's stock. You schedule a company valuation for some future date—or spell out a formula that will determine the stock's value. If the valuation or the valuation formula shows that your company's stock has risen by, say, $30 a share, you send the executive a $30,000 check. At tax time, your company qualifies for a $30,000 tax deduction, while your executive pays *(Continued)*

(Continued from page 85)

taxes on $30,000 worth of ordinary income.

Each year for 10 years at Wakefield Distribution Systems, senior vice president Gabrielle Fecteau, the employee whom Lucey considers essential to his business, earns "stock" equal to 1% of the company's assessed value. At the end of that time, she may cash out over a 10-year period, collecting not more than 10% of her accumulated value each year. And if Lucey—who owns the majority of the stock and whose children own the rest—at some point declares a dividend, Fecteau is entitled to a percentage equivalent to the amount of "stock" she has earned up to that point. Wakefield's accounting firm does an annual business valuation. Over the course of five years, Lucey says the value of the company—which had 1998 revenues of $18 million—has almost doubled.

Fecteau's continued presence is critical to Lucey's succession plan. His three children, ages 31, 30, and 25, are all involved in the business. "My son, Kevin, is managing a division of the company," says Lucey, "and I want to give him some time to mature and to learn the business from Gaby as well as from me. She has more time to teach and train than I do, plus, my son gets a different perspective from her." Lucey expects to be actively involved in the business for another three to five years and hopes that after that, his son and Fecteau will run it together. In the meantime, Lucey is quite pleased with his phantom stock—or, as he prefers to call it, mirror stock—plan. "It's the best way to incentivize key employees in a family-owned business or small business," he says.

Get the Scoop on Salaries

L ifeCare Assurance, a 150-employee insurance-plan administrator in Woodland Hills, Calif., used to make compensation decisions using a method long favored by small companies—educated guesswork. "We tried to go by what felt appropriate," says Carol Box, who oversees human resources at LifeCare. Then, however, 10 departing employees in a row all had the same complaint about LifeCare: skimpy pay. Box concluded that the company's pay scales might need adjusting. LifeCare, which had 1998 revenues of $8 million, needed to get some relevant salary surveys to find out.

Box is not alone in her interest in comparative salary data. Fortunately, a proliferation of salary surveys, many of them available over the Internet, is making that sort of benchmarking more accessible to small companies. Of course, big consulting firms sell hefty compensation surveys, usually at equally hefty sums. But these days, trade associations, chambers of commerce, the U.S. Bureau of Labor Statistics, and state and local governments are all sources of relatively inexpensive intelligence on market rates for compensation. You can also subscribe to a number of Internet services that will provide you with comparative job-price data, either on a one-time basis or for an annual subscription fee.

The danger of using any survey is that you might end up with the wrong numbers or you might analyze the numbers incorrectly. Behind every survey is a set of assumptions and criteria. If you are unaware of them, you could be comparing apples and oranges, or computer programmers with program directors. **Assessing the data in compensation surveys** can be tricky, but here are some key questions to ask. *(Continued)*

(Continued from page 87)

ᨊ *Are the companies polled comparable in size to your own?* Big companies, of course, tend to pay more than small ones. But the size of the disparity tends to be proportional to the job level. A chief financial officer will earn a lot more at a big company than at a small one. Data-entry clerks at both companies will probably make about the same amount.

ᨊ *Is the geographic focus appropriate?* Geography does not affect compensation for high-level positions nearly as much as for low-level ones. The reason? The job market for managers and professionals is national, while the market for blue-collar workers is generally regional, or even local.

ᨊ *How were the jobs "matched"?* A study is of little value if the jobs in question aren't comparable to one another. Simply matching them by title doesn't do the trick, especially in this day and age of cross-training, hybrid workers, and offbeat job titles such as "chief evangelist." For this reason, many surveyors are switching to so-called "maturity studies," which measure a worker's skill set rather than job description. In general, if a survey is based on in-depth, face-to-face interviews, the jobs will be better matched than if the survey is conducted by mail.

ᨊ *How old are the data?* In rapidly moving fields such as information technology, fresh information is of the essence. When assessing the age of a survey, consider when the salaries in question were put into effect, not when the survey was published.

ᨊ *How many companies were polled?* Experts say that a survey isn't credible unless it includes at least 20 organizations and discloses a full list of them in its report.

V

"If you use benefits to build a cadre of talented people who will stay with you for years and years, you'll hold on to your power. Your company's future will just get stronger and stronger."

LARRY LOKEY
founder and president,
Business Wire, San Francisco

45
IDEA

T.G.I.F.

In the early 1990s, a very promising job candidate presented David Mason with an ultimatum. The potential hire hesitated to join Mason's St. Louis architecture and engineering company, because changing jobs would force him to give up an attractive benefit. He had been **working extended days and taking every other Friday off**. "He spoke with such fervor, and we really wanted to hire him," recalls Mason, the president and CEO of David Mason & Associates. Though skeptical, Mason decided the peculiar schedule was worth a try at his company, which at that time had only three or four employees.

Now Mason's team of approximately 100 employees works daily from 7:30 a.m. to 5:30 p.m.—putting in 81 hours in nine days. On alternating Fridays, the company shuts down while a skeleton crew of five or six—who will get the following Friday off—holds the fort. And whoever works on Friday does not stay past 4:30. Most clients, Mason says, share his philosophy that "in the larger scheme of things, there's rarely a problem that can't wait until Monday."

Since he implemented the schedule, Mason reports "a dramatic change in the amount of sick time employees take. We've found that our productivity has increased, and we've got people calling us who want to work here just because of the schedule."

46
IDEA

Take Your Time

We were beginning to grow, and it was always tough when someone came to us and wanted time off," recalls Bill Liebegott, president of Hi-Tech Hose, in Newburyport, Mass. "We had to make a lot of emotional decisions." So Liebegott decided to take the subjectivity out of his company's time-off policy. All 50 hourly employees were given their own **paid-time-off (PTO) banks**. Liebegott's partner at the time, Jerry Feijoo, suggested the innovation because he had seen it work for his former employer, a large engineering firm. Hi-Tech Hose has since been acquired by a British company, United Industries, and the PTO account system has been discontinued. However, here's how the system worked successfully at High-Tech Hose, which reports annual revenues of $9 million.

During their first two years at the company, hourly employees banked 6.67 hours of time off with pay each month, for a year's total of 10 days. They drew from their PTO accounts to cover all absences, including vacation. The number of hours an employee accrued each month increased with seniority: A 20-year veteran, for example, earned 14.55 hours a month, or about four weeks a year. Employees could immediately withdraw from their PTOs or squirrel away the saved time indefinitely.

"Employees had choices for using that time off," says Liebegott. "They may have used it for vacation, personal time, or sick days, or just accumulated it. It was like a savings account—it was theirs forever." Once they had banked more than 80 hours, workers could redeem the excess hours by exchanging the hours for cash at the workers' current rate of pay.

The plan's flexibility eliminated any need for employees to tell white lies. And, Liebegott adds, "it took a lot of stress off the owners."

47

IDEA

Holiday Buffet

Employees were asking Howard Meditz, president of Marquardt & Roche/Meditz & Hackett, a marketing agency in Stamford, Conn., for an additional paid holiday. But he couldn't decide which holiday to give them. Plus, Meditz worried about closing the office on a day when some of his clients would probably be working. His solution? A **flex holiday plan**. At the beginning of the year, the company, which reported billings of $40 million in 1998, distributes a list of 23 holidays that includes everything from Saint Patrick's Day to Yom Kippur. Employees can sign up to take any 11—and one of their choices is a floating holiday whose date they can select. When the company hires new employees in the middle of the year, those employees start off by earning one holiday for each month they have worked with the company.

The agency's 35 full-time workers now have flexibility; they don't have to dip into vacation time for, say, religious holidays. Meditz, meanwhile, doesn't have to worry about clients not being able to get help when they need it. That's because within departments, some employees may work on a particular holiday while others don't, ensuring that the office stays open.

48

IDEA

Time Off for Good Behavior

When one of his most valued employees announced that she was quitting to hike the Appalachian Trail, Kurt Bleicken felt a pang of panic. So Bleicken, the CEO of GreenPages, a Kittery, Maine, computer-reselling company with 1998 revenues of $88 million, told the employee she could return to her job after she was done hiking. Several months later, the employee came back charged up and more productive. "I thought that maybe this isn't such a bad idea," says Bleicken. He now offers a six-week sabbatical, with full pay, to his 125 employees after five years of employment.

Bleicken isn't alone. These days employers and employees alike are thinking more about life-and-work balance. And companies conscious of the tight labor market are looking for ways to keep employees happy and productive over the long haul. While sabbaticals are hardly epidemic— especially among small companies—some growing businesses are starting to **offer longtime employees paid or unpaid periods of extended leave**.

In 1990, Michael May and his partners left Apple Computer to found Empower Trainers and Consultants, a training business in Overland Park, Kans., that had revenues of $10.8 million in 1998. None of them had been at Apple for the five years required to take advantage of its sabbatical policy. May says he regrets missing the opportunity, so he instituted a sabbatical policy at Empower. After three years of service, employees are eligible for two weeks of sabbatical that they can combine with one week of vacation time, for a total of three consecutive weeks off; after six years, they can similarly combine five weeks of sabbatical with one of their *(Continued)*

(Continued from page 93)

vacation weeks.

You might argue that the last thing a growing company can afford is to let staff members go off gallivanting for long stretches of time. "From an overhead standpoint, it's not cheap," May admits. In his business, "giving someone six weeks off could cost you $25,000 to $30,000 in lost revenue." But refreshed employees, he argues, are more creative employees, and that could enhance long-term retention and productivity. "This has actually saved us a bunch of people who had totally reached burnout," says May. Plus, the benefit helps bring people on board in the first place. "It's a differentiator that most firms don't have," he says. "We have a tough time competing for people if they just want the money."

Sabbaticals can disrupt a company's work flow, so May requires employees to give a minimum of two months' notice. What if an employee decides not to return? Both Bleicken and May admit that's a risk. But if that occurs, the reason goes beyond the sabbatical, May thinks. "If they weren't happy with what they were doing, they probably weren't as good at doing it."

49
IDEA

Fun and Gains

O nce a quarter, Mark Firmani closes his company for the day and takes his 10 employees to the movies. But not because business is slow. Firmani, president of Firmani and Associates, a public-relations firm in Seattle, says that the company, which has revenues of $1 million, has plenty of work. Just the same, four times a year the employees don their pagers, forward the phones to the voice-mail system, and take in a matinee.

Firmani claims he **shuts down for the day** to stay competitive in the market for good employees. Seattle is, after all, Microsoft country, and the local economic boom has attracted some big-name public-relations firms to the area. "There are agencies here that can charge big bucks and pay well above the national scale," says Firmani. "So I try to give this place a more enjoyable atmosphere."

To create that kind of atmosphere, Firmani uses more than just fun excursions. Other relatively inexpensive perks that Firmani has found effective include a weekly lunch for the whole staff, a casual dress code, and daily supplies of juice, soda, and candy. His PR professionals usually wear jeans, sometimes sweats. In fact, all that Firmani requires is that employees be within an hour of wearing something presentable in case a client drops by. "I keep a suit here at the office," he says. "Not that I wear it much."

We've Got You Covered

For Peter Hermann, health insurance is a headache. "Health insurance is a remarkably large expense, even for a 15-person firm like ours," says Hermann, a general partner of Heritage Partners, a private-equity investment firm in Boston. "You can't hire and retain good people without a good benefits package. But as managers, we need to spend an inordinate amount of time thinking about health insurance—not only because the costs keep rising but because the marketplace is so volatile. There's a forced need to keep reevaluating your company's coverage as insurers pull out of certain types of products or make other major changes."

What should you do when your company is faced with a health insurance rate hike? Obviously, you can shop for a new plan or increase employees' contributions. But what if you've already tried those options? While there isn't a miracle cure, here are some additional **strategies to help keep health insurance costs down**:

Isolate niche coverages. "Areas like prescription-drug coverage can nickel-and-dime you to death unless you set up a system that encourages employees to think twice before they make every single purchase," says Paul Gregory, a health insurance consultant based in New York City. So-called "behavior-health" coverage (such as psychiatric care and substance-abuse treatment) is another area that can jack up the cost of your company's coverage if you're not careful.

One suggestion is to remove those niches from your basic health-care plan when you are comparison shopping among insurers. Then contract for each of those niches with managed-care specialists who can fine-tune your coverage so that it remains a meaningful, but controlled, benefit for employees.

"It's amazing the way a well-planned copayment charge will discourage employees from using the company plan for every prescription drug they've ever heard of that might or might not turn out to be necessary," Gregory explains.

   ⁂ *If you're making cutbacks, introduce plan improvements at the same time.* "Most employees recognize that health-care coverage is expensive, so they're willing to make some trade-offs, especially in a situation where they feel they're also getting a real benefit or an improvement in their plan," notes Vincent Gandolfo, a senior managing director at Frank Crystal & Co., a New York City-based insurance broker and consultant serving middle-market companies.

It's also important to make sure that your cuts yield meaningful savings. For example, many businesses now have plans that offer employees some sort of choice between managed-care and traditional indemnity coverage. Gandolfo often finds that business owners who offer a choice try to lower costs by increasing the deductibles or copayments on the indemnity plan (which generally is the more expensive option for the employer).

"I hear it all the time from clients," Gandolfo notes. "They say, 'How can it be that you won't knock 10% off my costs if I'm willing to sign up for a $1,000 deductible on the indemnity coverage?'" However, Gandolfo says, it doesn't work that way. Insurers realize that most employees will sign up for the managed-care option, which means that's the place where you need to make meaningful cuts.

Gandolfo's recommendation for real bottom-line savings? Raise your managed-care copayment charge on "in network" office visits from, say, $5 to $10 or $15. *(Continued)*

(Continued from page 97)

✿ *Start aggressively monitoring all aspects of your plan.* Cost control is obviously one important aspect of plan monitoring, but other issues matter, too, such as the quality of the plan and the popularity of various features. It's much easier to negotiate cost-control measures when you know which coverages actually matter to your employees and which benefits are not meaningful.

✿ *Look beyond short-term price swings.* No matter how aggressively you want to control costs, it's not realistic to think that your company can switch insurance carriers every year or so, argues Jill Andresky Fraser, finance editor for *Inc.* magazine. She notes that just cleaning up the paperwork trail from holdover claims could overwhelm you. But, Fraser adds, you'll benefit by setting up a health-care strategy that takes into account coverage and cost-control goals over two to three years.

Her recommendations: Stay in touch with your insurance broker or consultant throughout the year to make certain your plan is keeping you on track. Be prepared to make annual adjustments to your existing plan(s) to respond to changes within the marketplace or your employee base. And of course, comparison shop among insurers every few years to find out whether a big switch makes sense.

51
IDEA

To Your Health

Who isn't sick of getting clobbered with huge hikes in health-insurance premiums? Since the early 1990s, Highsmith, a Fort Atkinson, Wis., supplier of library products with about 300 employees, has found a way to keep health insurance cost increases consistently lower than average. The secret? **Employee-health screening and an incentive-driven wellness program**.

Back in 1989, Highsmith's health insurance carrier informed the company that its premiums were set to increase 50%. Highsmith sprang into action, enlisting both a new carrier and its own workforce in a strategy that has lowered costs significantly over the long haul.

According to Bill Herman, Highsmith's vice-president of human resources, the company conducted an initial medical screening of its employees in 1991. The results of that screening suggested that unhealthy conditions, such as smoking, obesity, lack of exercise, high blood pressure, and high cholesterol, multiplied by intangibles like stress and back problems, were costing more than $250,000 a year in excess health-care costs. "We felt that some people would make healthy lifestyle changes for a carrot, and for many people, the carrot is money," says Herman.

So, the company initiated its Wellpower Plus program. The voluntary program gives employees and their spouses the chance to participate in annual screenings that measure such things as cholesterol levels, blood pressure, heart fitness, percentage of body fat, and general fitness. Each participant is assigned to one of three "incentive levels" based on the test results. Level one, the healthiest group, earns a 50% reduc-   *(Continued)*

(Continued from page 99)

tion in health-insurance premiums; level two saves 25%; and level three saves 12.5%. Herman says that 75% of employees who are covered by the company's insurance participate in Wellpower Plus. To help people achieve better health, Highsmith offers a number of on-site classes, on topics such as exercise, yoga, weight control, nutrition, and smoking-cessation.

But what happens to employees with hereditary or chronic conditions that preclude their assignment to a low-risk group? When the company assigns risk levels, it takes into consideration waivers that each employee's doctor may sign to certify physical conditions beyond that employee's control.

In recognition of the success of Wellpower Plus, Highsmith's health-maintenance organization has moved Highsmith from its community pool into an "experience-rated" arrangement. Since 1992, Herman says, Highsmith's annual increases in health insurance costs have been significantly lower than the HMO's population as a whole.

Herman reports that, by 1997, Highsmith's per-employee health insurance costs were only 68% of the per-participant cost for the overall HMO. And, when Highsmith's claims are less than expected, the company gets a rebate from the HMO. In 1997 alone, Herman estimates that the premium savings were about twice the cost of running the wellness program. "We really think our wellness program is paying off," he says.

52

IDEA

Gimme a Break

Life at an entrepreneurial company can be stressful. That's why increasing numbers of growing companies are offering workers some type of respite. For example, SAP Campbell Software, a Chicago-based company that has about 75 employees and makes workforce management software, has introduced a **stress-free zone** in its headquarters. In that area, employees are asked not to talk about work, according to Linda Tinoly, Campbell's manager of administration. Among the sanctioned activities: playing with the rotating inventory of toys, such as squirt guns and Velcro darts. "It gives people a place to go to decompress," says Tinoly.

Such facilities can start small. When Noble-Met Ltd. was founded in 1989, the company's recreational equipment consisted of a dart board, says John Freeland, Noble-Met's president. As the company grew, so did its recreational facilities. In 1998, Noble-Met reported more than $13 million in revenue, and its 4,000-square-foot break room included not only a dart board but also pool, air hockey, Foosball, and Ping-Pong.

"It gives people an opportunity to relieve stress," says Freeland. "We've never had a problem with people abusing the privilege." In fact, Freeland says workers at the company, which manufactures metal components for medical devices, actually police their colleagues' use of the break room more than management does. Freeland attributes this vigilance to the company's "aggressive" profit-sharing program. Employees know that goofing off doesn't contribute to the bottom line—or to their own share of the company's profits.

53

IDEA

Eat, Drink, and Be Merry

Want to improve *esprit de corps* at your company? Try eating together. GeoAccess, based in Overland Park, Kans., provides its workers with some unusual perks. It offers five fully **stocked pantries and has lunch delivered** every day. "The payoff is twofold," says Joy Weaver, the company's equivalent of a chief financial officer. (GeoAccess, which provides software and Internet services for the managed-care industry, uses no titles.) "First, it keeps people in the office, available for phone calls, and second, it helps develop camaraderie." It also helps with recruiting. Weaver estimates that the company, which has 190 employees, feeds about 100 of them on any given day at a cost of about $600 a day. The cost of snacks and beverages for the pantries probably adds about an additional $5,500 a month, she says.

There are also plenty of more modest approaches to sharing meals. For example, it's hard for a CEO to get to know all new employees when a company is growing. So every month or two, Randy M. Pritzker, CEO of Omicron Systems and Omicron Consulting, in Philadelphia, meets his companies' newest hires for lunch. There he discusses the history and philosophy of the businesses, which have combined sales of about $30 million. "This way they're more comfortable in the elevator and hallways because we're at least acquainted," he says.

54
IDEA

Shopping for Retirement

I t's not easy to find **retirement plans suitable for entrepreneurial companies**. Ask Brooke Dickinson, the president of Ditco, a Kent, Wash., company that designs and manufactures electronic-control systems for industrial equipment. Dickinson, whose company employs 15 people and logged revenues of $1.2 million in 1998, investigated 401(k)s and other retirement plans for about a decade before finding the right companywide plan. She and her husband, Jim Bitondo, Ditco's general manager, were convinced that "after health insurance, this was the most meaningful benefit we could provide." But the costs and complications kept scaring them off.

"We wanted to go with a 401(k) because we liked the borrowing option and wanted new employees to be able to roll over existing 401(k) savings into our plan," Dickinson explains. "But we kept running up against a big hurdle, which was the treatment of so-called highly compensated employees."

In 1998, when Dickinson launched Ditco's plan, those employees were defined as anyone who owns 5% or more of the company or earns more than $80,000. Regulations for standard 401(k)s restrict such employees' savings levels in proportion to those of lower-paid employees. Those restrictions, Dickinson says, "would have limited Jim and me to saving less than we would have with a regular IRA, which just didn't make sense."

In January 1998, Dickinson and Bitondo finally implemented a retirement plan: a SIMPLE 401(k), which was a fairly new option at the time. The two liked the SIMPLE 401(k) because it allows anyone in their company to contribute up to $6,000 a year, regardless of own-   *(Continued)*

(Continued from page 103)

ership status or salary. The payoff? In early 1999, all but one of Ditco's employees were participating in the plan.

Although the SIMPLE 401(k) works for Ditco, other companies may need different types of plans. Dan Maul, president of Retirement Planning Associates, in Kirkland, Wash., offers this advice on how to comparison shop for a retirement plan among insurance companies, mutual-fund houses, and other providers:

ஃ *Focus on identifying the right kind of plan for your company.* "Once you figure out the type of plan that works best and unbundle the services you're shopping for, it's remarkable how quickly everything else falls into place," Maul notes. Don't let yourself get bogged down with figuring out where you should invest your (and your employees') retirement savings, Maul urges. "You'll have millions of investment options. The thing to decide first is which type of plan is right for you."

ஃ *Unbundle the services you need.* "Companies basically require two types of services: the administrative ones—which include setting up the paperwork, filing taxes, and conducting compliance testing—and the investment services, which basically boil down to investing participants' savings," Maul explains. "Plenty of companies will offer to provide both services, but it's easier to compare costs and negotiate for lower prices when you've broken them down and shopped them separately."

ஃ *Get tough on investment costs.* "You need to compare investment options by breaking them down into three components: transaction costs (or what you'll be charged for buying and selling shares), ongoing operating costs (or the charge for servicing each account), and performance results."

IDEA

A Piece of the Action

Think your company is too small for a formal **employee stock ownership plan** (ESOP)? Maybe not. Bruce Pinsky, president of Packaging Consultants, in New Bedford, Mass., started an ESOP when the company had only six employees. When his partner died suddenly in 1989, Pinsky persuaded the estate to sell the partner's shares to the company's newly created ESOP. The ESOP option was financially beneficial to the heirs, and Pinsky thought the ESOP would rally his six employees, who were shaken by the death. It would "put our future in our own hands," he says.

Pinsky retained 51% of the stock; the rest went into what's called an ESOP trust. The trust, Pinsky explains, holds the stock and allocates it to employees' accounts, where it vests over time. When a fully vested employee retires, the employee's shares are bought back by the company. What's more, Pinsky says, when the company buys back a retiring employee's stock, that employee can roll the proceeds into an Individual Retirement Account (IRA) without paying taxes. "It's a very powerful wealth tool" for employees, he says.

Pinsky is sold on the motivational effects of his ESOP. "A lot of younger CEOs aren't fully aware that it can get lonely running a business," says Pinsky, who turned 44 in 1999. "You're vulnerable to employees' coming and going and hurting your ability to grow." The ESOP ties employees to the company and encourages them to "work and live their lives as if they were owners." Since 1990, the company, which designs and sells packaging, has experienced sales growth of 117%, and Pinsky's current staff of 12 have accumulated significant wealth as their stock has appreciat-   *(Continued)*

(Continued from page 105)

ed in value.

The tradeoff is that Pinsky gave up equity in his company. But, he stresses, "if it were just me against the world, trying to manage people conventionally, we never would have achieved that growth.

"Owners rise to challenges better than employees, particularly in a small company," Pinsky notes. The ESOP has been a strong incentive, he says, by improving employee loyalty during difficult times.

That improved loyalty doesn't come automatically, however. "You have to work at it," Pinsky emphasizes. "You have to continue to educate and remind" employees about the ESOP's benefits. The best kind of reminder? "We had our first ESOP owner retire," Pinsky says, and that meant employees got to witness a colleague reaping the benefits of her stock ownership. "She is a living example of what happens at retirement."

Are you interested in ESOPs? While he was exploring the ESOP option, Pinsky says he consulted his lawyer, his accountant, his pension actuary, and the National Center for Employee Ownership, in Oakland, Calif. (510-272-9461, or www.nceo.org).

56

IDEA

Retire in Style

Here's a shocker: According to a 1997 study by the accounting firm Coopers & Lybrand (now PricewaterhouseCoopers), the most common executive perk in America is something called a SERP. Never heard of it? The term broadly refers to all kinds of **"supplemental executive retirement plans"** that provide deferred compensation to key employees and business owners. The study found that 60% of the 149 companies surveyed had some type of management SERP.

Small companies, however, make little or no use of SERPs. "They tend to offer stock options instead, which managers have viewed as an attractive substitute," says survey author Carl Weinberg, a principal in PricewaterhouseCoopers's Westport, Conn., office. But, Weinberg warns, that may change if stock market conditions make options less profitable. Then, "smaller companies won't be able to compete with bigger corporations for top talent unless they start offering SERPs as well."

Although SERPs don't earn the same tax benefits that you can get from "qualified" companywide retirement plans such as 401(k)s, the "nonqualified" plans, such as a nonqualified profit-sharing plan for selected employees, don't bring the same regulatory hassles, either. With nonqualified plans, you can pretty much offer whatever you want to your highly compensated employees. Just remember the trade-off in tax benefits: Although your business's contributions to a qualified plan result in current tax deductions, your company's contributions to a nonqualified plan will not provide tax deductions until people actually receive the funds. Note: To set up a nonqualified plan, you will need expert professional advice.

57

IDEA

Home with the Kids

Donald Fay, operations manager for the Payne Firm, a Cincinnati environmental consulting firm with 1998 revenues of $4 million, has begun to tap an underused labor source: stay-at-home parents of small children. Fay now allows these employees to **telecommute while working part-time**. "Seven years ago," says Fay, "it would have been hard for me to get past the idea of paying someone who's not in the office." But after spending thousands in recruiters' fees, he realized that offering the flexibility of telecommuting and part-time work enabled him to keep valuable employees. "In today's labor market, you need to be flexible to keep good people," Fay says.

Payne's part-time at-home workers submit time sheets electronically and get their work assignments via voice mail and e-mail. Some other Payne employees, Fay says, also periodically work at home to increase productivity. "That's something we encourage," he says.

Making Convenience Count

When Connie Swartz began hiring employees in 1989, her fledgling consulting firm in Kansas City, Mo., couldn't afford hefty salaries and fancy benefits packages. But Swartz, whose company provides training development and software documentation, had something that a growing number of employees value even more—flexibility. She gave her employees **flexible hours and the ability to work from home**, plus a strong say in their budgets and how they're compensated.

"If my kids are sick," says instructional designer Mary Lee, "I'm able to be with them during the day and do my work after they go to bed."

Swartz's company, Creative Courseware, which has four employees and annual revenues of nearly $1 million, still doesn't have a formal benefits package, but that's because employees have voted consistently for increases in wages (everyone is paid by the hour) as opposed to, say, health insurance.

And since good communication is vital to her company's success, Swartz works hard to keep everyone informed and encourages employees to do likewise. Employees use e-mail, fax, and phone to communicate with one another. Every month, Swartz distributes notes on clients and the status of proposals. She holds formal staff meetings as needed and hosts an annual three-day, off-site retreat at which the group discusses long-term strategy, compensation, the company's financial position, and so on.

Swartz also schedules an annual "review day" with each employee, where the two of them talk about the employee's performance and spend some time together. All this communication seems to pay off: In the past seven years, Swartz has only lost two employees.

59
IDEA

Look Before You Lease

Mark Pahmer, president of 22-employee Graphics for Industry, in New York City, is a big fan of **employee leasing**. That's because employee leasing results in less expensive health-care premiums and a broader range of benefits choices for the employees of his company, which provides 3-D graphic services to ad agencies and film production companies.

What's employee leasing? An employee leasing company—often known as a "professional employer organization" (PEO)—will take over technical human-resources administration for the company that hires it. In doing so, the PEO becomes a co-employer of the company's workers, charging a per-person fee based on the client's employee count.

The arrangement is a win-win situation. Employees win because PEOs can often offer a broad range of benefits at lower cost because they are the co-employers of so many workers. Graphics for Industry wins, says Pahmer, because his accounting staff can focus on collecting receivables instead of, say, doing payroll and sorting out insurance claims. He explains that the PEO now takes care of those tasks and nearly every other technical and legal human-resource task as well.

Pahmer, who began using employee leasing in the early 1990s, has had a happy and profitable experience, but had he been dealing with a less reliable PEO, things might have turned out differently. The employee-leasing industry has seen some spectacular flameouts, owing to everything from bad risks and poor management to outright fraud. When a PEO goes under, its client companies often discover that their payroll cash and insurance coverage also vanish. If you are considering a PEO, here are some criteria to help you decide if the one you are considering—or the one that is seeking your business—is right for you.

• *Financial strength.* Zero in on the company's economics. Demand to see *audited* financial statements, and have an accountant dissect them for you. Some PEOs, in rushing to lock up as many clients as possible, take on risky accounts that can undermine their financial stability. The soundest PEOs are selective in accepting new business.

Determine if your state licenses PEOs that meet certain standards. Also check with the Institute for the Accreditation of Professional Employer Organizations, in Little Rock. This self-regulating industry group has accredited only 21 or so PEOs to date, but they represent workers in 50 states. Find out more at the Institute's Web site (www.iapeo.org).

• *References.* Request a long list of the PEO's clients. When you call them, concentrate on details: With whom inside the PEO do you deal? How often do its staffers visit your site? What happens when there's an injury? A lengthy list of clients helps ensure that you won't get just references who are schooled in the "right" answers, and it offers a wider look at the PEO's customer base.

• *The comfort zone.* When you take on a PEO, you're taking on a partner. Check for a personality fit. You and your employees need to feel comfortable with the switch. Employees are invariably skeptical at first, but a good PEO will offer orientations to alleviate their concerns. Also, make sure the PEO's executives have clean records.

• *Services.* Ask if the PEO will customize a program to your requirements. If you want to administer your own 401(k), for instance, the PEO shouldn't object. But if you want too narrow a slice of its services—say, only workers' compensation insurance—it might not want you.   *(Continued)*

(Continued from page 111)

Miriam McKendall, an employment lawyer in the Boston office of Holland & Knight, advises that you ask if the PEO will defend and indemnify you against employee lawsuits relating to the services it is responsible for.

✒ *The merger possibility.* Be aware of the potential for a merger. Several years ago, the employee-leasing firm that Mark Pahmer worked with was acquired; he now works with the successor PEO. "It wasn't a problem," Pahmer says. And he notes that mergers make sense in the industry because "it's a volume-buying business."

✒ *The contract.* If the PEO hands you a standard contract, remember that "everything is negotiable," says McKendall. Be wary of signing anything that broadly insulates the PEO from liability. Some PEOs, McKendall says, will try to slip in potentially pernicious clauses. It's a good idea to have an employment lawyer review the contract.

VI

"I always have my cell phone, a pager, and of course e-mail, but sometimes I think it's personal communication that's missing."

RANDY SCHILLING
CEO, Solutech,
St. Charles, Mo.

Ask Me Anything

Michael May, CEO and president of Empower Trainers and Consultants, an Overland Park, Kans., training company that had 1998 revenues of $10.8 million, truly believes in honest communication. To underscore that point, May holds voluntary staff meetings at which **anyone can ask the boss anything**—business-related or personal. Empower staff members who work in other offices participate in these meetings through conference calls.

To keep the meetings on track, May limits each person to only one question. After he writes everyone's questions on a board, he begins answering them. That way, the meeting can't be sidetracked by one individual with many questions on the same topic.

May believes that without such meetings, "the rumor mill becomes the method of communication" that dominates a company. He finds that these forums not only keep communication clear but also help him connect with his people. "It keeps me on my toes, as well," he says. One big challenge: convincing people new to the company that there will be no reprisals if they ask the CEO tough questions. "It's essentially a search for truth," says May.

61 IDEA

Open Books

Labor-management relations were strained at Cin-Made when Bob Frey and his partner purchased the Cincinnati-based company in 1984. The situation deteriorated further when Frey won a 12.5% wage decrease from employees. He felt he needed the decrease, but, not surprisingly, employee morale plummeted. In order for his business—which at the time made paper tubes and paper canisters—to succeed, Frey realized he needed the cooperation of his workforce. One way he hoped to accomplish this was by opening channels of communication.

Frey **instituted open-book management**, a system that teaches employees about the financial performance of their company so that they understand how the business makes money. But that's not all. In an open-book management system, employees are given a stake in the success of the business. For example, Frey introduced a profit-sharing program that, by the late 1980s, accounted for about 25% of employees' compensation. Finally, employees are encouraged to find ways to improve the company's performance.

"In effect, open-book management teaches people to quit thinking of themselves as hired hands (with all that implies), and to start realizing that they are businesspeople (with all that implies)," writes John Case, author of *Open-Book Management: The Coming Business Revolution* (HarperBusiness, 1996). "Their job security, their chances for advancement, their hopes for the future all depend not on the whims of some boss or department head but on the company's success in the marketplace and each person's contribution to it."

(Continued)

(Continued from page 115)

At Cin-Made, open-book management changed employees' adversarial attitude toward management. The process was very slow at first. Over time, however, hourly workers at the company began taking on new responsibilities; today they have a say in areas such as Cin-Made's hiring process and safety program. The company has grown, too. In 1995, Frey says Cin-Made had 40 employees and about $3 million in sales; in 1998 it had about 100 employees and sales of about $8.5 million. And, with less labor-management conflict, Frey finds that work has become enjoyable.

Implementing change can be easier in a company in which employees and management see themselves as part of the same team. By the mid 1990s, Frey recounts, Cin-Made had few prospects for growth in its existing business, so employees and management alike voted to reinvent the company. "If you're going to have long-term career potential, this is something we must do," Frey remembers telling employees before the transition.

That change—which has meant launching new divisions with new products—has complicated open-book management a little, because entering new markets has temporarily hurt the company's profitability. During the transition, Frey is offering employees a guarantee of a portion of their normal profit-sharing income. He has also started a quarterly incentive program based on improving particular areas of the company's performance. That way, employees will continue to focus on helping the business run better.

Show Them the Money

Like all CEOs, Jay Goltz was painfully aware of how expenses can whittle away profits. "I'd spend all day looking at bills and think, 'If my employees only knew what it takes to keep this place going,'" says the president of $10-million Artists' Frame, in Chicago. Meanwhile, he suspected his employees were studying invoices for pricey framing jobs and wondering, "Why aren't we making more money?"

"It occurred to me that employees had no idea what workers' compensation costs or what I spend on advertising or rent," says Goltz. So, he decided to **demonstrate the business's cost structure**—in a way that they all would be able to understand.

Goltz gathered his 110 employees for a role-playing session, during which vice-president of operations Mitch Gabel posed as a customer with a $100 framing job and Goltz represented the company. Using a fistful of oversize dollar bills, Gabel handed over increasing amounts of "cash" as Goltz itemized the expenses that went into attracting the customer and completing the job.

"What do you think our advertising costs?" Goltz asked the employees. "It's $50,000 a year, or about 5% of each job." Gabel relinquished $5. Then he watched his stack of money shrink further as Goltz continued collecting for health insurance, maintenance, rent, materials, labor, the telephone, and so on.

When Goltz was finished, Gabel was left with a paltry $5. "It was easy for employees to see that the difference between making money and losing money is sliver thin," says Goltz. "I wanted them to get   *(Continued)*

(Continued from page 117)

perspective on the expenses that aren't obvious to them and to use that information to make better decisions. For an hour's worth of time, I couldn't ask for a better payoff."

Goltz is not the only CEO to find this method of communication effective. Prakash Laufer, CEO of Motherwear, a Northampton, Mass., catalog company, did a similar exercise with employees, starting with an average net sale of $100. Laufer then broke the sale down to show how much of the $100 went to each line item on the company's income statement and how much was left over in pretax and after-tax profits.

In August 1997, when the company had $5 million in sales, Laufer held a meeting to celebrate the fact that, instead of losing $3.23 on that typical $100 sale (the spring 1996 figure), Motherwear had raised it to a profit of $11.23. Laufer attributes that turnaround partly to the original expense-breakdown exercise.

Everybody's 2¢ Counts

As an entrepreneur, you may have all kinds of great ideas, but you need employee buy-in to implement them. That's why Jennifer Lawton, CEO of Net Daemons Associates, headquartered in Woburn, Mass., and now part of Interliant, makes sure her 55 **employees have access to the company's strategic business plan**, which is updated annually. Lawton posts the plan on the company's intranet and solicits employees' feedback. At an annual offsite meeting, the entire staff of the computer-network consulting company, which had 1998 revenues of $5.5 million, gathers to review next year's strategy and hear about the previous year's performance.

As an added incentive, the offsite meeting offers a chance to "get everyone together to meet each other and have some fun," Lawton says. "It's a great way to energize everyone all at once." At that yearly event, employees are expected to ask questions and offer suggestions. "Our employees are very vocal," says Lawton. "If they don't pipe up there, they will follow up with you independently."

Lawton has demonstrated to her employees that she pays attention to their comments. At one annual meeting, an engineer questioned the 100% to 200% growth projection for the upcoming year. After a lengthy discussion with the staff, Lawton changed the projection to 80% to 100%. "His question caused me to think about how that growth feels from an engineer's perspective," says Lawton. She decided to grow the business more slowly, rather than risk alienating her employees.

64

IDEA

Enough, Already!

CEO Andrew Sather and his partner, Chris DeVore, director of business development, figured that to make their four-year-old strategic Internet consulting company, Adjacency, into a powerhouse, they would have to tap the entrepreneurial instincts of every staffer. In 1998, they started meeting with their 25 workers weekly to discuss the details of the San Francisco-based company's operations, including cash flow and potential customers.

The partners could tell that workers appreciated the honest communication. But it quickly became apparent that there were **some things employees would rather not know**. For instance, they didn't want to hear about Adjacency's close calls with missing payroll. Such near-misses are not uncommon in the entrepreneurial world, but they're unnerving to employees. "We overestimated our employees' desire to be entrepreneurs, and sometimes we scared them," Sather says. The partners now avoid discussing the nitty-gritty cash-flow details.

Sather and DeVore also overestimated their staff's ability to keep secrets. In one meeting, they told employees about a potentially lucrative deal with a hot new client. One worker left the meeting so pumped that he bragged to a friend at a competing company. The "friend" relayed the news to his bosses, who promptly tried to persuade the coveted customer to dump Adjacency and go with them. "We almost lost the client," DeVore says. "The client was livid, and rightfully so." Adjacency subsequently grew to 80 employees and was recently acquired by Sapient. The partners are now more careful to identify which information is top secret. "We've learned to get a lot more explicit about how information can be used," Sather says.

65
IDEA

Perfect Partnerships

Wesley Phillips, CEO of the Hunter Barth advertising and marketing agency in Costa Mesa, Calif., was surprised to hear employees gripe about the strategic partnerships he had formed with outside market-research, direct-marketing, and public-relations agencies. Hunter Barth employees "would get angry if projects went slowly, and they didn't always use the new partners when there were opportunities to do so," says Phillips, who had sales of $7.2 million in 1998.

Once he **instituted systems to promote harmony with partners**, Phillips found that things improved. He asked the partners to adapt to his company's way of doing business by making requests in writing and sending finished work on disks compatible with Hunter Barth's computers. Other changes included holding regular meetings between his employees and the partners' staffs as well as having the two groups make joint presentations to customers.

Sharing information with partners is critical. But you also have to be cautious about how much you divulge. Kathleen Mullinix, chairman and CEO of the biotechnology company Synaptic Pharmaceutical, in Paramus, N.J., instructs her employees in how to manage her company's alliances with large drug companies such as Eli Lilly and Merck. "We have separate groups of people working with each partner," says Mullinix, whose company had revenues of $9.3 million in 1998. "Scientists love to talk about what they're doing, but they're told that the partner should get information only about the specific project we're working on," she says. That policy is critical: The pharmaceutical giants must be confident that their proprietary information isn't finding its way to a competitor via their smaller biotech partner.

"We don't write down much. We have a rule that people in the branches must read the first memo that arrives in their offices from the corporate office each month. After that, they can wad up the memos and shoot 'em in the can."

PATRICK KELLY
founder and CEO,
PSS/World Medical, Jacksonville, Fla.,
and author, with John Case, of
*Faster Company: Building the World's
Nuttiest Turn-on-a-Dime, Home-Grown,
Billion Dollar Business*
(John Wiley & Sons)

66
IDEA

Talking Up a Storm

What's the most valuable resource a business can have? It's a supply of ideas—more specifically, good ideas. So how do you generate them? **Get your best and brightest people in a room and brainstorm** your way to riches. The key is to allow communication to flow freely.

In cold reality, however, brainstorming sessions are often more storm than brain, producing useless ideas and much boredom. But it doesn't have to be that way, according to Gerry Tabio, senior vice-president in charge of the creative-resources division at Chancellor Media Group, a radio-broadcasting company with headquarters in Dallas. Tabio has made a study of brainstorming, using his findings to help Chancellor, its affiliate radio stations, and advertisers generate new ideas for everything from station promotions to sales campaigns. He says that many corporate brainstorming sessions end up being abortive or acrimonious because the participants don't follow these simple ground rules:

🍋 *Stress quantity over quality.* You want to generate as many ideas as possible. "The purpose of brainstorming is to make a list before you make choices," Tabio says. What brainstorming sessions aren't for is discussion. "In discussions people walk out with the same thing they came in with," he explains. "All they do is defend what they already believe. No one learns anything." Encouraging quantity forces those with agendas to think beyond their pet ideas. "By generating a list, people can still write down the opinion they brought, but then they have to come up with more," he says.

🍋 *Suspend judgment.* In the session no one is allowed to criticize an idea or discuss why it isn't feasible. "Our favorite pastime is to   *(Continued)*

(Continued from page 123)

talk about what isn't going to work," says Tabio, "which is completely worthless. Every single idea expressed in a brainstorming meeting should be written down, no matter how dumb it may sound at first."

❧ *Don't set limits.* Tabio says the totally outlandish should be not only allowed but encouraged. "The wilder and more outrageous the ideas, the better," he says. "That's how you get the really useful, unexpected ideas. Creativity comes from being willing to play and to consider alternate possibilities." Tabio recommends taking the group on mental detours. "Ask questions that put the task in a new context," he says. Say you're looking for some ways to jazz up an all-staff celebration. You might ask the group, "How would Steven Spielberg spice up this party?" Answer: He would use a video camera to record people's impressions and play them at the event. "Detours revive a stalled brainstorming session when the list gets boring," he says.

❧ *Ignore seniority.* People aren't going to freewheel in a meeting in which they have to please the boss, so for the purposes of the session, everyone has the same rank. Sure, eventually someone must be held accountable. But Tabio recommends that the "problem owner" should wait until the session is over before exerting any authority. "During the session you're only useful to me if you're generating ideas," he says. "People know when there's someone in the room with veto power."

67
IDEA

Reach Out and Touch Everyone

Rusty Childress, president of Childress Buick-Kia in Phoenix, Ariz., believes in communication. At this car dealership with 105 employees and 1998 revenues of $35 million, Childress has instituted a number of **programs to improve communication within the company**. They include:

≈ *Childress College.* Childress wants to make sure that all the departments work well together, so new recruits at the company go through a seven-week orientation program designed, he says, "to build empathy" for one's colleagues. During the orientation, dubbed "Childress College," new employees spend one day a week in a different department. They also learn about the concepts of "internal customers" and "internal suppliers." At the end of the training, employees sign a pledge that says they know who their internal customers are.

≈ *Take-Five Meetings.* To tap employees' ideas, Childress periodically picks five workers at random and asks them how they would improve the dealership.

≈ *Employee-Satisfaction Index.* For a more systematic approach to communication, Childress conducts a survey of employee satisfaction twice a year. The survey also asks employees how well they think management is doing and how the owner might do things differently.

As a result of all these communication programs, Childress has found that his employees' customer-service performance has improved, as measured by the dealership's customer-satisfaction ratings. His programs have also made it easier to recruit and keep employees.

REAL
WORLD

"A good way to reinforce
the work ethic in your
workforce is to circulate
stories about efforts
above and beyond the
call of duty."

WILL PAPE
cofounder, VeriFone,
Santa Clara, Calif.

IDEA 68

Questionable Situation

Connie Swartz, president and CEO of Creative Courseware, has never liked traditional performance review forms. After she founded her Kansas City, Mo., company, which develops customized training curriculums and provides software documentation, Swartz gradually **developed her own model for performance reviews**. Swartz's model is based around two sets of questions, one for Swartz and one for the employee under review. The questions are designed to start a dialogue between Swartz and the employee— one that Swartz finds "more useful" than a more traditional review. "What comes out of it is what we need to change," says Swartz, whose company has five employees and racked up nearly $1 million in revenues in 1998.

Swartz's system is probably not for everyone; many entrepreneurs, for example, value having data such as numerical performance rankings on a rating scale, because such ranking can help measure performance and document problems. However, even if you use more traditional performance review forms and are happy with them, Swartz's questions could add an interesting, thought-provoking element to your review system.

Here's what Swartz asks the employee to tell her.

- *What accomplishments are you most proud of, and why?*
- *What have you learned this past year?*
- *What are the most frustrating things about your job?*
- *If you could change one thing about your job, what would it be?*
- *What can I (the boss) do to help make your job easier/better?*
- *If you were I, what one change would you make in our company?*

(Continued)

(Continued from page 127)

And here are the questions that the employee gets to ask the boss.

    During the past year, which of my accomplishments are you most proud of, and why?

    What do you like best about the way I (the employee) do my job?

    What are the most frustrating things about how I do my job?

    If you could change one thing about my job, what would it be?

    What can I do to help make your job easier/better?

    What do you feel are my roles and responsibilities, and how do they fit with your vision of where Creative Courseware is going?

Because many of her employees work from their homes, Swartz also uses each review as an occasion to strengthen her relationship with them. The performance review day generally starts at 10 a.m., and Swartz does not schedule anything else that day. The employee gets to choose a place to go for lunch at the company's expense. By making sure to leave plenty of time for conversation and dialogue, Swartz tries to make her performance reviews anything but perfunctory.

IDEA

My Door Is (Almost) Always Open

An open-door policy—under which employees may approach a manager when his or her office door is open—sounds like a great management idea until the reality of a busy day intrudes. "I want to be available and accessible, but I really hate you for interrupting me," is how Jim Lucas, president and CEO of Luman Consultants, a 15-employee company in Shawnee Mission, Kans., describes the feeling that stressed managers can easily convey to employees. To avoid giving similar mixed messages, Lucas, who has written three books on the leadership and management in the workplace, decided it made more sense to use a "modified open-door policy." Under his system, the **position of his office door serves as a signal**.

"An open door means come in; I truly am available. A partially open door means I'm pretty busy, but come in if it's really important. And a closed door means I'm about to explode; come in if it's a life-threatening emergency," Lucas explains. "Using the door as body language cuts out all the baloney."

70
IDEA

Reality Check

In these days of information overload and virtual offices, it becomes harder and harder to get your employees' attention. If they are seldom all in the office at the same time, how do you communicate company news effectively? You can send an e-mail, but will all employees read it? Many high-tech phone systems allow you to send out a voicemail blast to all users, but will everyone listen to it?

At Synergy Networks, a network-integration business in Vienna, Va., which had 1998 revenues of $10 million, CEO Mark Gordon wanted to make sure he communicated effectively with the company's 50 employees. But, reaching them was tricky; some didn't work in the main office, for example, and some took forever to check their messages. So Gordon decided on a time-honored solution—a brief, biweekly company newsletter. Better yet, he found a way to make sure it gets noticed: The **newsletter is stuffed into employees' pay envelopes**. "Everyone gets a paycheck," Gordon observes. "And they tend to open those."

"**P**eople will put their hearts and souls into a company if they think the owners are putting their hearts and souls into it."

TIMOTHY P. HENDRICKS
general partner,
T.H. Properties,
Franconia, Pa.

71
IDEA

Picture This

At Cincinnati-based Kendle International, the company's headquarters feature a special kind of art—photos of employees. The pictures, which were originally part of an ad campaign, feature employees posing happily with symbols of their favorite activities, from scuba gear to grandchildren. Chairman and CEO Candace Kendle found that displaying the photos not only boosted morale and a sense of belonging among employees, it also made the company more inviting to prospective hires.

"By recognizing the lives of our employees outside the workplace, we recognize our workers as people," says Kendle, whose company grew explosively from 288 employees in 1997 to 1,089 as of spring 1999. This contract research organization, which serves the pharmaceutical and biotechnology industries, is in the process of sharing the concept of a **workers' photo gallery** with its other offices in the United States and around the world.

Another entrepreneur, Herb Kelleher, cofounder of Southwest Airlines, also believes in the power of pictures. "In the hallways of our headquarters, we have photos of our employees—about 1,500 pictures of our people engaged in various activities, being honored, given awards," says Kelleher. "Those pictures show that we're interested not in potted palms or in Chinese art but in our people."

72
IDEA

Everyone Can Play

How can you build employee teamwork and loyalty to your company? CompuWorks, a computer systems integration company based in Pittsfield, Mass., found that it helps to **give employees lots of ways to get involved** in the company. "People wanted to feel that they were part of something larger," says Brenda Wilbur, former COO of CompuWorks, which had sales of $5 million in 1998. "They wanted to feel that their peers relied on them to do their best, day in and day out."

CompuWorks must be on the right track. The company has been named four times to the annual *Inc.* 500 list of the country's fastest-growing privately held small companies. And in an industry rife with job-hopping, Wilbur says annual turnover at the company never exceeded 5%. Here some of the ways CompuWorks invites employees to participate:

❧ *Decision making.* Some employees serve on the company's advisory board; they are elected by people in their departments and are paid $50 for each meeting they attend. The company's charitable giving efforts are managed by a community involvement group; the annual "fun" budget, which covers everything from nights out at the movies to the annual family retreat, is controlled by a social activities group. "This level of involvement gives people a real say in what's happening," notes Wilbur.

❧ *Information.* Meanwhile, in the "Ask Al" section of the CompuWorks intranet, employees can post any question anonymously to company president Al Bauman. Bauman then posts his responses for debate. The company also tries to engage employees on a personal level by offering in-house seminars, listed in the biweekly company newsletter. *(Continued)*

(Continued from page 133)

Topics can range from relieving stress to getting a better deal on auto insurance.

   ❧ *Recognition.* Here, too, employees have a big say. The "Wizard of the Week" award is presented to the employee who goes beyond the call of duty. Employees nominate peers, and the winner is chosen by the reigning Wizard. The award: a quirky statuette, a book, and a $50 gift certificate.

   ❧ *Financial management.* CompuWorks teaches employees how to read key financial statements and then challenges them to work on fictitious statements, so as to become familiar with the process. Once that's clear, they start developing their own departmental scorecards, which some departments update weekly. Service and software employees, for example, chart billable hours, while software trainers watch attendance rates in their classes. The administrative staff watches cash-flow levels. Eventually, most sales reps' commissions will be eliminated so that everyone can focus on the big picture: profits. CompuWorks employees not only receive regular bonuses based on company profits but also gain a palpable sense of personal achievement. "Individuals can see clearly how valuable they are to our organization," says Wilbur.

73
IDEA

Truth or Consequences

No one wants to tell the boss an unpleasant truth and risk his or her displeasure. But in today's ultra-competitive markets, increasing numbers of savvy entrepreneurs are trying to help their organizations improve by **cultivating employee feedback**. After all, the thinking goes, it's better to have your employees tell you you've got a problem now than to have your customers tell you later.

"Hierarchy is, to a large degree, a thing of the past," notes Richard Block, CEO of Impac Group, a fast-growing company that designs and prints packaging for a range of consumer and entertainment products. Still, Block adds, there's a "stifling tradition" that prevents people from communicating what they really think.

How can you learn employees' true opinions? It helps if you:

ᴥ *Create opportunities for anonymity.* At CompuWorks, a computer-systems-integration company based in Pittsfield, Mass. (see previous idea, "Everyone Can Play"), the 65 employees can ask the boss whatever they want, anonymously on the company intranet.

ᴥ *Don't ever "shoot the messenger"* by penalizing employees who bring out painful truths. At Raymond Karsan Associates, a human-resource-services firm in Wayne, Pa., Rudy Karsan knows that employee grumblings often signal opportunities for this fast-growing company, which projects 1999 revenues of about $75 million.

Karsan takes every chance he can to encourage employees to criticize him. At quarterly meetings with top staff, Karsan initiates a discussion about his behavior and his blind spots. He also takes one of *(Continued)*

(Continued from page 135)

his 450 employees out to lunch every quarter and runs gab sessions, at least quarterly, for 10 employees who sign up for the privilege of castigating him. The process has helped identify problem areas, from unclear communication to Karsan's failure to greet people in the morning. Karsan says the most important thing he can do during the fault-finding process is shut up. "If you try to be defensive," he says, "you're dead in the water." And there can't be any repercussions for employees' honesty, either. "If there are," he says, "word spreads quickly and the process becomes useless."

Reward honesty and tough questions. By 1998, the revenues of Impac Group, a company in Melrose Park, Ill., that does special printing and packaging, had grown to $280 million—in part by out-inventing its competitors. Its culture, CEO Richard Block explains, maintains that creative edge by promoting open debate and the combustible rub of ideas—"an environment that is for experimentation and that urges you to take responsibility for a problem instead of working at concealing it." To underscore that principle, Block submits to lively interrogation at employee meetings and rewards his toughest questioner with a prize. The message: Nothing is sacred. Questions are good. We're all—CEO included—accountable to one another.

74

IDEA

All Ears

Customer service at EconoPrint in Madison, Wis., was in chaos in 1992 after the company consolidated eight separate printing facilities into a centralized production operation serving eight quick-print shops. "When the customer-service person couldn't walk to the back room and explain something to the press person, it became a nightmare," says co-owner Dave Roloff. If orders were unclear, jobs were either done incorrectly or left until morning, resulting in lost revenues.

After a number of miscommunications between the print shops and the production center, Roloff and CEO Patrick Leamy **enlisted employee input**. They asked the administrative employees to help draw up a survey that was given out to the staff, then 60 people. It asked workers for information such as "the five biggest obstacles to doing your job correctly." Next, individual departments met with Leamy and Roloff to discuss how to improve customer service. Afterward, an informal election was held, with each department selecting one person to represent it at the next interdepartmental meeting. At first, says Roloff, the meeting "was pure ugliness. It had nothing to do with customer service and everything to do with wanting to get things off their chests."

Once the air cleared, the group got down to work. It consisted of 15 employees, at various levels of seniority—even some recent hires, who were helpful, says Roloff, because "they wouldn't all say, 'We've always done it this way.'"

The first task was to design a one-page customer-order form to help solve the company's communication and workflow prob-   *(Continued)*

(Continued from page 137)

lems. The representatives were asked what they needed to know to answer every question their individual departments might have about an order.

The customer-order form was so effective in detailing the work process that today, out of the roughly 6,000 jobs that EconoPrint completes monthly, fewer than 25 exhibit problems. Tighter controls at the newly centralized operation have meant greater net profits. Profits rose 34% in 1993 and have risen steadily every year since, according to Roloff. In 1999, EconoPrint had 150 employees and projected revenues of $14 million.

EconoPrint has found employee ideas so helpful that after the first initiative, the company involved employees in other major changes. In 1995, management solicited employee input as EconoPrint sought to automate the entire order-taking process. All 120 employees filled out a questionnaire that asked, among other things, what they would change at work. EconoPrint also got employee input on a more recent automation plan, and the company later consulted its workers about their ideas for a planned move to a new facility.

Roloff believes that seeking ideas from everyone has helped the company grow—and has helped reduce employees' resistance to major changes. "Once you hit implementation, there's incredible buy-in," he says.

75
IDEA

Please Complain

The devil," the old saying goes, "is in the details." And sometimes it's your employees who know the details of your business. It's not always easy, however, to get employees to speak up and make suggestions that could improve your company's performance. "People are hesitant to complain," observes Mark Gordon, CEO of Synergy Networks, a 50-employee network-integration business in Vienna, Va., which had 1998 revenues of $10 million. "They don't want to be perceived as negative."

Gordon came to that realization when his employees were reluctant to fill out a form to report hassles that interfere with their job performance and to suggest solutions. So Gordon added a new component: Now these "hassle reports" are collected weekly, and a drawing is held every three to four weeks for everyone who has submitted a hassle. The winner of the drawing can select a modest prize from a catalog.

Gordon is willing to **reward employees who complain** because he's found that undetected problems can cost his company money. For example, people who worked in the field reported the following hassle: They had to return to headquarters to recharge a certain piece of equipment, because the company only owned one battery charger. Synergy Networks had been losing thousands of dollars in productivity as employees fruitlessly drove back to the office to recharge their equipment. Gordon reports that the problem was easily alleviated by buying additional chargers that only cost about $100 each. However, without a system to encourage employee complaints and suggestions, he adds, "there was no way for that kind of stuff to bubble up" from the ranks and get managers' attention.

76 IDEA

The Measure of Morale

So many managers believe you can't measure morale," says Jack Stack, CEO of Springfield ReManufacturing Corp. (SRC), a Springfield, Mo., company that overhauls truck parts. "That notion is not only wrong but dangerous. What gets measured gets done. If you don't measure morale, you wind up taking it for granted. You don't focus on it," says Stack, whose company had 1998 sales of about $150 million.

Employee morale isn't taken for granted at SRC any more. In 1996, one of SRC's subsidiaries took part in **a survey of employee morale** conducted by the Gallup Organization for *Inc.*'s 1996 "State of Small Business" issue. The results were so intriguing that SRC decided to modify the survey, adapting 14 of the questions to suit its own needs. SRC management then distributed the new surveys to all its other subsidiaries and asked employees to complete the forms anonymously.

The results were surprising. Notably, SRC's Heavy-Duty division, one of the company's most profitable subsidiaries and one that Stack considered "the crown jewel of SRC," had very low scores in three areas. For example, 43% of the employees in the division disagreed with the statement, "At work, your opinions count."

What was the matter? Management at Heavy-Duty decided to recruit volunteers for an employee-satisfaction committee. Eighteen people, representing all departments and shifts at the division, joined the new committee. Its mission: to improve Heavy-Duty's scores in the problematic areas of the survey.

It wasn't hard to find the problems, Stack recalls. Even a member of the committee said he didn't feel his opinions counted at work. He described a simple problem that affected his work that he had been complaining about for two years, with no resolution. The committee was able to remedy the situation the next day.

"It soon became clear that we didn't have two or three big problems at Heavy-Duty," Stack observes. "Rather, we had loads of little problems, most of which could be solved quickly and inexpensively just by bringing them to the surface and focusing on them."

SRC learned its lesson. Now, the company conducts an employee morale survey every six months—and tracks its employee morale data religiously. For Gary Brown, SRC's corporate director of human resources, the data help indicate what's working, and what's not, at the company. "It gives me a gut feeling for what's going on out there," he says.

For example, if an unusually high number of employees in one department indicate on the anonymous survey that they are looking elsewhere for work, that might mean a supervisor there is alienating employees. "At least it tips you off: There's something rotten here," says Brown. Similarly, if some part of the company shows a continual decline in morale over the course of two or three survey periods, Brown knows he should find out more about the situation. He has also found that responses to a survey question asking employees whether they are looking for work elsewhere can be used to help predict the company's turnover rate.

In general, SRC has had good success with using employee focus groups, such as the one used in Heavy-Duty, to solve problems that the survey identifies. And the company has made some significant changes based on issues raised by the survey. For example, Brown says SRC has altered some of its training for supervisors by increasing the emphasis on showing concern for employees. That's because Brown has *(Continued)*

(Continued from page 141)

discovered that a crucial survey question is the one that asks whether a supervisor or someone at work seems to care about the employee as a person. If employees indicate that no one seems to care about them as people, Brown observes, they are likely to answer other questions negatively, as well. "They want someone to care about them," he concludes.

Supervisor training isn't the only thing that's changed at SRC. Survey results helped management realize that many employees didn't understand the mechanisms for moving up in the company's ranks. Now, Brown says, the company has changed its annual performance review form, called an employee annual report, to include a section on individual career planning.

All in all, the surveys have taught SRC management a lot. Not the least of the lessons is just how easy it is to be ignorant of many employee concerns. "There are problems out there we don't even know about," Brown says. "It is a continual learning experience."

77

IDEA

Company Report Card

n the early 1990s, Alan Lewis struggled to create a mission statement for his travel company, Grand Circle Corp. The final document outlined the Boston-based company's responsibilities to "our customers, our associates [read employees], our stakeholders, and our world." But by the mid-1990s, the demands of the company's rapid growth had made it difficult for Lewis to gauge how well Grand Circle was living up to those lofty ideals. So he queried the folks who knew best. Lewis **asked employees to grade the company** in each of the four areas covered in the mission statement.

Lewis found the exercise so helpful that it's now repeated two to three times a year at the company, according to Grand Circle communications director Priscilla O'Reilly. A survey is sent via e-mail to all employees, and they are asked to grade the company on its performance in the areas of responsibility to associates, responsibility to customers, financial responsibility, and social responsibility. The results are tabulated and brought to the senior management team, along with a summary of the issues that employees raise as they complete the "report card." That senior team, O'Reilly says, chooses the top issues in each area, makes some decisions about how to address them, and then reports on those decisions at a company-wide monthly meeting.

Management's report also goes into the company newsletter, O'Reilly notes. For example, in 1997, employees gave the company a "B" in financial responsibility—the major issue raised was control of the company's general and administrative (G&A) expenses. "You've said that leadership needs to be more accountable and that departments should *(Continued)*

(Continued from page 143)

know and stick to their budgets," management reported in the company newsletter. "Beginning in 1998, departments are responsible for their own G&A expenditures, with detailed budgets, monthly reviews and outlooks, and accountability of functional heads."

Grand Circle employees aren't exactly easy graders. For example, in the fourth quarter of 1998, employees gave the company a "B-" in every area except social responsibility, where the company earned an "A." O'Reilly explains that the company's corporate culture is "very critical—the idea being that negative criticism is really positive." Indeed, the criticism highlights issues that are important to the business—such as a need to upgrade the company's computer systems and to improve the company's ability to predict call volume.

Grand Circle is certainly doing something right: The company has grown substantially—from about 230 employees in 1995 to about 600 in early 1999, O'Reilly says—and revenues reached $228.2 million in 1998.

78
IDEA

Grading the Bosses

For almost 120 years, Hyde Manufacturing found that top-down management worked just fine. But in the late 1980s, when foreign competition began heating up, the Southbridge, Mass., manufacturer of hand tools and machine knives decided to shift to a team-based structure in order to become more flexible.

It wasn't easy, however, for the family-owned business, which had 1998 revenues of $40 million, to convince shop-floor supervisors that leadership no longer meant ordering people around. But, a new feedback system that **gives employees the opportunity to review their team leaders** has smoothed the transition. Hyde's human-resources director, Dick Ayers, got the idea for this upward review system after doing some reading in the company's library and hearing a speaker at a conference.

Under the team-based organization, Hyde's shop-floor supervisors had become "facilitators." Ayers knew they understood machines but not necessarily how to manage: "We had to convince them that it's important to address other areas, like how to motivate people." Because he wanted the upward review to be constructive, he decided not to tie the results to compensation.

Hyde started in November 1994 with a pilot program involving six teams, ranging in size from five to 20 shop-floor employees. Each team met with training manager Doug DeVries, who explained the exercise and the evaluation categories and handed out the one-page review questionnaires. Within half an hour, the reviewers had completed the forms. DeVries tallied the results, shredded the original forms to preserve anonymity, and scheduled meetings with the facilitators *(Continued)*

(Continued from page 145)

who had been reviewed, to discuss the results.

A second review, held in November 1995, involved almost all of Hyde's 308 employees. Shop-floor workers reviewed their facilitators. Those team leaders then rated their business-unit leaders, who in turn assessed the director of manufacturing operations. Ayers was reviewed by his subordinates, too. "None of us scored as well as we thought we would," he says. The big message from workers to bosses: "Be visible and be more involved."

Although team members welcomed the chance to give input, the exercise met with a mixed reception from the facilitators. Ayers estimates that 20% loved it, 20% loathed it, and the rest felt they could take it or leave it. Overall, however, the results have been positive. Hyde's reduction in voluntary turnover (12% in 1998, compared with 26% in 1989) is due in part to improved morale. Also, employee input has helped the company become more efficient.

After a number of workers reported that facilitators were difficult to reach in an emergency, the company stocked up on $300 two-way radios, one for each facilitator and one for each team. The investment produced a surprising additional payoff. Hyde runs emergency drills three times a year, and on a good day without radios the company could evacuate the plant in 10 minutes. Now, with the aid of the radios, everyone is out in three and a half minutes.

Ayers says the company, which repeated the upward review in 1997, found that the exercise also helped identify some ways in which the company needed to provide facilitators with better training. He thinks that Hyde will do the upward review again, but he also thinks it's important to allow ample time between reviews. Some employees find the upward reviews unsettling, and it takes time for real changes to occur. "It's not something you do every year," he concludes.

Group Gripes—and Kudos

At the Motley Fool, an on-line investor-education company based in Alexandria, Va., the company intranet offers a team forum for constructive criticism that can help employees improve their performance. Using a program called "Stop, Start, Continue," the company's 125 employees were asked in November 1998 to assess one another's job performance and comment on the work habits of coworkers. Tom Conner, a Web developer at the company, says using the intranet encouraged more honesty, especially when it came to offering frank opinions to superiors he might otherwise have been reluctant to confront.

Here's how the Motley Fool system worked: Employees clicked on a coworker's name in a particular section of the company's intranet, then wrote suggestions regarding specific habits that person should stop, start, or continue. The comments were forwarded verbatim to department coordinators, who were instructed to keep all complaints anonymous.

Managers filtered the input back to employees. That meant the **intranet peer feedback system** added new duties to those already placed on company managers—who spend a lot of time with workers in one-on-one conferences. But "I don't mind," says information-technology coordinator Dwight Gibbs, "because peer feedback is still so much more valuable than a top-down evaluation."

The Motley Fool plans to use the system again, possibly doing three rounds of evaluations a year. This intranet "suggestion box" will operate independently of the company's official annual review process, through which promotions are decided and awarded. The idea is to help employees improve their performance by bonus time.

Personality Plus

When it comes to recruiting, Dale Van Aken, a software developer in Langhorne, Pa., relies on standard methods. "If you interview well, it's not that hard to gauge how candidates would test anyway," he says. If he excluded a job applicant on the basis of test results, Van Aken says, he'd fear that he was throwing the baby out with the bath water. However, along with numerous other CEOs, he has found psychological tests to be most valuable after an employee is brought on board.

These days, increasing numbers of entrepreneurs are **using personality surveys to help existing employees work together** more effectively. Van Aken, CEO of Syncro Technology, uses a well-known psychological instrument called the Myers-Briggs Type Indicator (MBTI) to promote communication and team creation at his company. The Myers-Briggs test characterizes a person using one of 16 types. Each type consists of a four-letter code designed to reveal key attributes of the respondent's behavioral style. For example, one of the four letters is always either an "E" or an "I" (reflecting either extroversion on introversion).

Van Aken says that Syncro Technology, which has about 40 employees, has been using the Myers-Briggs since the early 1990s, and everyone in the company has taken it. "No one's ever objected to taking it," he says. "And we certainly wouldn't insist if they did."

At Syncro, the results of the MBTI are freely shared and used to help people of different personality types understand each other's behavior. Van Aken feels grateful to have the additional information to help him understand employees. "It's not an assessment tool; it's a communication tool," he says. "It's almost what we used to call sensitivity training."

Mark Gordon, CEO of Vienna, Va.-based Synergy Networks, which had 1998 revenues of $10 million, also uses psychological tests to help him understand employee behavioral dynamics. Gordon is so sold on these tests that at all times he carries minigraphs of the test results from each of his staff members.

He says the testing came in handy, particularly when his network-integration business merged with a network-cabling company in 1996. The tests helped Gordon map out the company's restructuring and put people in the right positions. "It was important that we retain the [cabling company's] management team and have it mesh with my team effectively," he says. "But, we wanted the rest of the employees to feel comfortable, and while we had the opportunity, we wanted to craft a position around them."

For example, Gordon points to two employees who at merger time did pretty much the same job—managing field personnel, which included recruiting, training, and scheduling staff, plus managing projects day-to-day. Those employees also handled pre-sale requirements, which involved establishing customer needs and rendering the bids. When he decided to split the field manager position into two distinct roles, he used the personality profiles of the two individuals involved to help him figure out how best to divide the duties between them.

Still, the transition after the merge was hardly tension free. Gordon admits that when the companies first merged, the atmosphere was "them" versus "us." So, the entire management team sat down with consultant Bill Wagner, who discussed, among other things, the groups' personality profiles. After the managers' group session, Gordon says, the situation was a lot better. And, for Gordon, understanding the emotional needs of each employee is a bottom-line business issue: When employees *(Continued)*

(Continued from page 149)

are content, they tend to be more productive.

It can also be tricky to introduce the use of personality assessment tools. When Gordon first began using the tests in the mid-1990s, he made their use voluntary. After a few people took them and got their results, many more employees volunteered. Gordon notes that although most employees accept the surveys, some people have been put off by them. He also urges employers to realize that there are a number of different testing tools that yield similar insights. In 1998, for example, Gordon switched his company from one brand of testing tool to another. The new brand yields a lengthier report that he thinks managers can use more easily.

Let's Do (Free) Lunch

GeoAccess, based in Overland Park, Kans., provides its workers with five fully stocked pantries and has lunch delivered every day. The payoff from **having employees eat together** is twofold, says Joy Weaver, the company's equivalent of a chief financial officer. (GeoAccess, which provides software and Internet services for the managed care industry, uses no titles.) "First, it keeps people in the office, available for phone calls, and second, it helps develop camaraderie." It also helps with recruiting. Weaver estimates that the company, which has 150 employees, feeds about 100 of them on any given day, at a cost of about $500 a day. The cost of snacks and beverages for the pantries probably adds about an additional $3,000 a month, she says.

If your company can't afford this kind of outlay, try more modest approaches to sharing meals. For example, Randy M. Pritzker, CEO of Omicron Systems and Omicron Consulting, in Philadelphia, knows it's hard for the head of a growing company to get to know all the new employees. So, every month or two, Pritzker meets his companies' newest hires for lunch. There he discusses the history and the philosophy of the businesses, which have combined sales of about $30 million. "This way they're more comfortable in the elevator and hallways because we're at least acquainted," he says.

82

IDEA

Self-Rule

Sure, sometimes you ask your employees for input on issues related to human resources. But would you turn your HR department over to them? Believe it or not, some companies do, and **employee teams manage all or part of human-resources functions**. Some companies merely supplement a traditional HR department with representative committees. And some have gone all the way, eliminating the HR department entirely.

Bill Palmer, president and CEO of Commercial Casework, a Fremont, Calif., woodworking and cabinetry shop that had 1998 revenues of $10 million, practices the partial approach. He put together a group comprised of seven volunteers and himself to research and design the company's bonus plan. Palmer says not only did he get good information about how to motivate his employees, but his employees gained an understanding of the bonus process. "They learned a whole lot more about what it means to give and get a bonus," says Palmer. "They saw how difficult it was and wound up really taking ownership of the process."

Each year Palmer asks for a new group of volunteers. As he refines its membership and dynamics, the group "becomes another training tool," he says.

Similarly, at Com-Corp Industries, a 125-employee metal-stamping shop in Cleveland, 10 to 15 employees volunteer to serve for two years on the Wage and Salary Committee. The committee uses industry surveys to help determine the market rate for the type of jobs the company offers, according to Com-Corp president Tom Stanciu. And, if an employee disagrees with a performance review, he or she can take the grievance to the Human Resources Assistance Committee, which, like the Wage and Salary

Committee, is employee-run.

While Palmer and Stanciu have employee committees taking on some traditional HR functions, Martin McConnell went all the way. McConnell is vice-president of finance for Spectrum Signal Processing, a hardware and software designer based in Burnaby, British Columbia, with 180 employees and 1998 revenues of US$26 million. He says his company has no HR department at all. Instead, it uses rotating HR committees.

In a 1996 employee-satisfaction survey, Spectrum's managers discovered that its employees were not very happy with the way human-resource issues were dealt with in the company. So, Spectrum created a cross-functional employee team to focus on those issues. McConnell initially thought the committee would be only short-term, that it would deal with the immediate problems and then disband. "But, it gained so much interest and momentum, it became part of our culture," he says.

The committee regularly addresses most typical human-resources functions in the company: performance appraisals, the employee handbook, training, recognition, mentoring, and orientation programs. (Payroll and benefits administration are handled by the accounting department.)

The committee consists of 12 elected members from various job functions. Terms are staggered, so the committee is constantly getting new members and fresh perspectives.

McConnell and CEO Barry Jinks also serve on the committee in an advisory role. According to committee chairperson Carol Schulz, the bosses' presence is not a hindrance. "They have no more say than anybody else," says Schulz. And their presence "gives employees the feeling that they really do care."

McConnell admits that at first he worried the committee might establish some overly expensive policies. "But it's not us versus *(Continued)*

(Continued from page 153)

them," he says. "Whatever decision they made would be modified for what works for the environment. Or, maybe we'd implement it in stages."

Palmer of Commercial Casework has had a similar experience. He stresses that at his company, the employee group has limited power. "It's called an advisory committee," he says. "We made it clear that when they make decisions, they need to get buy-in from all the employees, that it has to be beneficial to the company, and mostly, that I have to buy it, too."

McConnell says one big problem is enlisting committee members without distracting them from their regular jobs. So, in 1997 McConnell and his group took on a co-op student from a local university to do the committee's legwork. That has worked so well that the group is currently assessing the appropriate timing for bringing on a full-time human-resources specialist.

"We'd definitely like to have somebody eventually," says chairperson Schulz. "But whoever we get will work side by side with the committee. The pro will bring strategic expertise committee members don't have."

83
IDEA

Successful Succession

One test of a great team is how well it functions after its leader steps aside. A good succession plan can eliminate many problems, but drawing up and following such a plan is a challenge in any business, particularly in a family business. Statistically, fewer than 10% of all family businesses make it to the third generation. Still, Camp Echo Lake, a family-owned summer camp in Warrensburg, N.Y., has a better chance of survival than most. "I know the odds are against us, but we're going to give it a shot," says Tony Stein, codirector of the camp that his grandparents founded.

Tony's father Morry was determined to **prepare his successors for ownership of the business**. "In the mid-1980s, we started having monthly or bimonthly family-business meetings," says Tony. "None of us were in the business then, but Dad felt it was important to keep us abreast of what was going on." As the family discussed everything from capital projects and pricing to estate planning, the role of each of the three sons emerged naturally. The oldest, Eric, was the outside adviser. The youngest, George, was impassioned by sales, and Tony, the Wharton M.B.A. with four years of outside experience, gravitated toward the administrative and financial duties. Morry Stein prefaced many of those meetings with the grim scenario, "If I ever die in a plane crash, here are the steps you need to take."

Eerily, that's exactly what happened in October 1994. "When my dad died, I knew exactly what to do," says Tony. "He had been training us for 10 years; those meetings were like fire drills." So far, the transition has been smooth, and George and Tony have purchased a majority of the camp from their mother—a succession tactic that was discussed at Morry Stein's meetings.

84
IDEA

Face to Face in Cyberspace

Caroline Davis, president of a women's clothing company, has surrounded herself with a stellar management team. Well, not literally. Davis's Worth Collection, which had $40 million in revenues in 1998, is based in New York City. But her three vice-presidents are in Indiana, South Carolina, and New Jersey. "I've always looked for the right person, regardless of location," says Davis. Moving key executives to pricey Manhattan would have cost the company a small fortune, so she decided **to make long-distance managing work**. Here's how she does it.

Hiring. "Worth hires people who work well independently and don't need constant supervision," says Davis. As part of the hiring process, she uses a written "personal profile" test for insight into prospective hires' work habits.

Communication. "Everyone is connected by electronic mail, voice mail, and fax so that communication flows much as it would in a single location," she says. "There are also weekly conference calls with all levels of management." Recently, for instance, the group discussed plans for a national sales meeting and a major recruiting effort. Managers come to New York every 10 to 12 weeks for additional long-term strategic planning.

Culture. "We pay more attention to our corporate culture than if everyone were in one place and we took it for granted," says Davis. On the phone, "sometimes we'll discuss a book, or I'll send out a magazine or newspaper article and ask for opinions on how it might relate to our own strategic planning." She adds, "Biweekly, Worth puts out a newsletter that goes to everyone in the company as well as to our independent sales associates. It contains everything from motivational pieces and corporate stories to letters we get from customers."

Like Davis, Will Pape has years of experience managing employees who are in distant locations. As co-founder of VeriFone, Pape helped grow that company as a "virtual corporation" with employees scattered across the globe. (VeriFone, which makes electronic payment systems and is based in Santa Clara, Calif., was acquired by Hewlett-Packard in 1997.) Here are Pape's tips for making long-distance management work:

🔊 *At least some of the time, have managers operate in cyberspace,* rather than out of the main office. "Sitting in a central office without plugging into the virtual culture is almost a guarantee of failure," Pape says. "You don't know what's going on, and you signal your employees that operating virtually isn't really important." And, like Worth's Caroline Davis, who brings her managers together regularly for strategic planning, Pape believes it's important for employees to get together frequently.

🔊 *Make sure home-based employees have appropriate work space.* "In my experience, one of the main causes of productivity decline in virtual organizations is inadequate work space," Pape observes. "Physical work space is so important that companies should provide written guidelines for home offices." He thinks every home office should be a separate room, with a door that shuts. It should also include at least two dedicated business phones lines—one for business calls, and one for e-mail and faxes. "When people put their office space where household functions go on—the kitchen table or the bedroom, for example—they have a hard time taking a break from work," Pape says. "In time those workers become bone-weary, and their productivity slumps."

🔊 *Strengthen relationships between remote workers and employees at the main office.* "People who work out of their homes or at cus-   *(Continued)*

(Continued from page 157)

tomer sites also need to spend some time in an office with their colleagues," Pape argues. "Any face-to-face meeting—a regular status meeting or an annual, sales, or planning meeting—is an opportunity for cross-fertilization." His tip: When you plan the agenda for a meeting that includes remote workers, allow extra time so employees can socialize. "Some managers are bound to wonder if such organized socializing is a waste of money," Pape notes, "but I believe that forging those ties creates both a sense of belonging and the personal relationships that are necessary for remote employees to work effectively."

☛ *Find ways to help people feel connected to the organization and to one another.* Make sure, Pape advises, that remote employees receive frequent—perhaps even daily—updates about company progress. Include them in planning initiatives, and make your corporate mission and vision clear to every employee. "When you become a virtual organization, your staff suddenly loses all those interactions in the hallway, in the elevator, and by the water cooler that help move projects forward and smooth out conflicts," Pape says. To compensate, he suggests making regular use of videoconferencing and telephone conversations. Relying on e-mail too much, he finds, can allow conflicts to escalate. "When workers do most of their communicating by e-mail, small irritations easily grow into major conflicts," Pape says. "Learning how to disagree remotely is an important component of being able to operate virtually."

"Too many small-business owners don't make time for the one employee incentive that will never break the company budget: Timely, honest praise of workers who do well. Research has shown that appreciation from managers is one of the incentives workers want most."

BOB NELSON
founder and president,
Nelson Motivation,
San Diego, Calif.

That's Entertainment

Who says business can't be fun? At OOP!, a specialty gift store in Providence with annual revenues of $1 million, owners Jennifer Neuguth and David Riordan maintain a light-hearted atmosphere in their store by **regularly orchestrating offbeat workplace celebrations**. Thanks to a book called *Chase's Calendar of Events* (published annually by NTC Contemporary Publishing Group), OOP! has celebrated everything from National Hug Month to country singer Willie Nelson's birthday. (On that day, the staff wore bandannas.) Riordan says the celebrations attract customers to the store and keep employees happy.

With the right attitude, even staff meetings can become celebrations. At Childress Buick-Kia, a car dealership in Phoenix with 105 employees and 1998 revenues of $35 million, president Rusty Childress holds a company meeting once a month. He has shifted the original focus, so that in addition to information about the state of the dealership, the meetings also address employees' need for recognition. At each meeting, any employee who has recently been recognized by customers or colleagues for good service is given a chance to spin a large wheel, reminiscent of the roulette wheels on TV game shows, to select a prize.

A typical monthly meeting generally includes about 10 minutes of quick updates from the company's five departments—followed by about half an hour during which 20 to 30 employees spin the wheel. The prizes they win aren't fancy. "We tend to go to Price Club and get the kind of food people like," Childress explains. While the event is playful, it also underscores a serious business message: the importance of good service.

86
IDEA

Monday Morning Magic

Weekly staff meetings can be deadly dull, but not at The Phelps Group, a marketing agency in Santa Monica, Calif., that posted 1998 revenues of $37 million. CEO Joe Phelps has found ways to **make the company's meetings lively** as well as informative.

The weekly ritual starts every Monday morning at 9:28, when Phelps goes on the public-address system with a "two-minute warning." Each of the firm's 56 associates heads for an all-purpose room. The carrot for prompt attendance is the first item on the agenda: a $100 bill to the person whose phone extension is drawn at random—if he or she can correctly answer a question from the employee handbook.

The meetings themselves move through the same five agenda headings each week. After the drawing, the second agenda item is for the company's teams—advertising, direct marketing, production, and media—to show off their new works. The third is to announce important agency or client business. The fourth agenda item, "Minutes," reinforces the need for brevity. Each of the teams delivers a one-minute mini-lesson, teaching the group about some key piece of expertise or perhaps summarizing a helpful article.

The last agenda item: the Atta Boy/Atta Girl award. This wooden plaque, festooned with personal effects (pennies from the company controller, a Pez dispenser), is awarded each week. The current award holder selects the next recipient and passes on the plaque.

"It's great to have a group experience at the beginning of the week," Phelps says. And it helps counterbalance the increasingly technology-enabled workplace in which there is less and less face-to-face contact.

87
IDEA

Rethink Employee of the Month

Although they are popular motivational tools, employee-of-the-month programs don't always improve employee morale. Just ask Dale Hageman, CEO of an employee-leasing business in Oklahoma City that had 1998 revenues of $123 million. Hageman feels that his long-abandoned employee-of-the-month program at Accord Human Resources wound up being "more negative than positive."

When managers selected honorees, Hageman says, some employees viewed the winners as teacher's pets. And when he attempted to involve peers in the selection process, many griped that the program felt like a popularity contest. "I thought it was very fair," he says. "But with these things, perception is reality." So, Hageman scrapped the program, opting instead for a less formal procedure: Each month, managers select outstanding employees for verbal recognition at a companywide meeting.

Kurt Bleicken agrees that it pays to **consider people's feelings when designing an employee-of-the-month program**. "You have to be careful how you do these things," says the president and CEO of GreenPages, a computer reseller in Kittery, Maine, that had 1998 revenues of $88 million. "They can be a real downer." After living through numerous problematic incarnations, Bleicken thinks that he's found a system that works. As part of the monthly selection process, each of Bleicken's sales teams picks a support-person-of-the-month, while each of his support teams picks a salesperson-of-the-month. Bleicken feels that the two-way voting procedure creates a mutually supportive atmosphere. "There is usually no dissension about who should have gotten what," he reports.

Play Money, Real Rewards

At the management-consulting firm IdeaScope Associates, top performers get more than a pat on the back. They might be rewarded, for example, with a certificate for art supplies, a party for the office, or skydiving lessons. **Employees purchase various perks with play money** that they earn when coworkers recognize them for doing outstanding work.

Criteria for awards are based on five factors key to the company's success, such as delivering excellent consulting and reaching the company's profit goals. Every month, says the president, Bob Krinsky, nominated employees each receive $25 to $100 in "IdeaScope Dollars" to use toward more than 60 possible prizes. A list of nominees is e-mailed to all 25 employees at IdeaScope's two locations in San Francisco and Boston. Each time an employee is nominated, he or she wins an award.

Many of the gifts, notes Krinsky, "provide people with experiences that give them a refreshing outlook on life and stimulate creativity." That fits nicely with IdeaScope's corporate mission, which is to help clients focus on strategic innovation and growth.

In real money, the company invests from $5,000 to $10,000 in the program each year. Krinsky thinks that's money well spent. "We value teamwork, shared risk taking, and experimentation," he says.

Vice-president Kim Kelley notes an unexpected benefit: The IdeaScope Dollars program has helped strengthen relationships among employees in the company's two offices, which are separated by an entire continent. The recognition program, Kelley observes, has served as "a mechanism that helps us think of ourselves as one organization that happens to have two locations."

Share the Salami

In 1995, Steve and Diane Warren, co-owners of Katzinger's Delicatessen, in Columbus, Ohio, attended a seminar on open-book management, a system that involves teaching employees about a company's financials and sharing the rewards with them when the company's performance improves. Sounds like a good policy, right? But, the Warrens found it difficult to implement.

As soon as he got back from the seminar, Steve Warren shared the financials of his company with Katzinger's managers. Despite his opening the company's books, Warren saw food costs—which he wanted to keep below 35% of sales—continue to grow. He realized he would have to tinker with the typical open-book strategy. "The restaurant business is different," he says. "Some of our workers are young kids who aren't so responsible because they don't have a mortgage to pay. Plus, turnover is pretty high."

Rather than focusing on the company's big financial picture, the Warrens decided they would present a short-term, simple goal that could energize their young, mobile workforce. In August 1996, they made a proposal to their employees—help us **reduce food costs, and we'll split the savings with you**. There were only two rules: Don't sacrifice food quality or portion size, and make sure that customers get the service they require.

It worked. "Our costs got in line immediately, and consistency improved," Steve Warren says. At the end of a year, Katzinger's had indeed reduced its food costs to below 35% of sales, saving $30,000 in the process. Steve and Diane Warren happily distributed $15,000 of that to their 45-member staff and began cooking up a new game aimed at increasing sales. By 1998, Katzinger's revenues stood at $2 million.

A Moving Experience

Ken Hawk's rechargeable-batteries mail-order business had outgrown its tiny location in a former grocery store in Silicon Valley. Given the high price of real estate in the area, Hawk wanted to relocate farther afield. He also wanted to keep as many of his 28 employees as possible, in order to be able to "hit the ground running" at his new site. "Who knew how many of them would go with me?" he says. "I was afraid I would lose half."

It turns out Hawk had nothing to fear. When 1-800-Batteries (now called iGo) relocated to Reno, Nev., in June 1997, an impressive 24 of his 28 employees eventually made the move, a fact he considers a vote of confidence in his company. (As of spring 1999, the company had approximately 100 employees.) In its new location, Hawk says, iGo's rent is half the price per square foot that it was in Silicon Valley, and the business pays no inventory tax. Hawk **moved his company without losing its best, highly trained people** by continuously motivating his staff and by:

• *Keeping communication open.* Hawk was very honest with his staff members. He informed them of the move as soon as he started planning for it—six months before it happened. When he had narrowed the possible locations down to two, he asked his employees for their opinions. "People advised us against telling employees about the moving plans, for fear they'd start looking for new jobs," Hawk says. "But I didn't think it was fair not to tell."

• *Maintaining a sense of excitement.* Hawk drew up a bulletin board with the layout of the new, larger building superimposed   *(Continued)*

(Continued from page 165)

on top of the original site. As people committed to moving with the company, Hawk posted their photos on the bulletin board. "It was kind of corny, but it helped get the momentum going," he says. He also offered a moving bonus and up to $850 in moving expenses to each employee— even to those he could easily replace. His theory: In a small, close-knit company, people's friendships with one another form an important motivation to relocate.

   Seeking economic-development help. Hawk credits the state of Nevada, and in particular the local economic-development agency, with making the move as smooth as possible. The state promised immediate residency for employees so that they could take classes at state universities at lower tuition rates. It also helped employees' spouses find jobs. "All but one spouse had a job when we moved here," says Hawk. "And she had to wait only because she's a nurse and had to get certified."

Shoe-in

Silicon Valley is notorious for its fluid job market in which workers move from company to company. That can make it hard for small companies to retain valuable employees. However, Latitude Communications, a telecommunications company in Santa Clara, Calif., which went public in 1998, has found ways to keep annual turnover among its 140-plus employees to a respectable rate of around 5%. In the opinion of CEO Emil Wang, one key factor is **a warm welcome expressed in tangible ways**.

As soon as new hires join Latitude, for example, Wang lets them know they are part of a community. Each new employee receives a T-shirt signed by other Latitude employees. "I put my T-shirt in my cubicle, and it no longer felt empty," says marketing manager Ning Peng. Latitude also tries to make the first day at work memorable. On that day, a new employee receives a $75 gift certificate for a pair of running shoes as a reminder that Latitude wants employees to put themselves in the customer's shoes.

In addition to the shirt and certificate, Latitude also sends photos of new employees to their spouses and offers new hires one week off to do volunteer work.

The 90-Day Checkup

Although it's nearly a cliche, it's hard to criticize the principle that the best way to satisfy your customers is to satisfy your employees. Still, it's one thing to advocate such a policy in a company and quite another to make it a reality. Quinton Studer, president of Baptist Hospital, a 5,000-employee facility in Pensacola, Fla., has done both. When Studer arrived, Baptist's admissions were flat, and patient satisfaction, as measured by a national survey, was slightly below average. Studer has used **rigorous goal-setting and measurement methods** to make the hospital more effective at satisfying both its employees and its patients.

Studer went to Pensacola in June 1996, after a stint as senior vice-president at Holy Cross Hospital in Chicago. He spent the next several years at Baptist developing a management model based on his previous experience as a special-education teacher. "Maximizing an organization's ability is similar to maximizing a child's potential," Studer says. "The first step is to diagnose the situation and then set achievable goals. The higher the goals, the closer the student or organization comes to reaching full potential. Every 90 days the teacher does an individual education plan to ensure that all resources directed to the child are aligned with the goals. And at the end of a year, old goals are reassessed and new ones are set."

Studer believes that measurement, as well as goal setting, was key to the improvements Baptist achieved. "We decided we had to have a measurable service goal," he says. "I believe you have to measure what's important to you, and that you have to have some means of comparison." While that's the basic plan, Studer has refined his system over the years and brought it to the point where it could be replicated, not only in other hospitals but also in any service business.

In Baptist's case, management met with all the employees and talked about the hospital's purpose, its reason for existing. "Everyone at the hospital said that they wanted to be the best," Studer recalls. "Becoming the employer of choice also became a goal at Baptist." Here's how Baptist rates patient and employee satisfaction plus employee performance:

❧ *Patient satisfaction.* Baptist began measuring patient satisfaction, using an outside company to conduct the survey. "The results help us set specific goals," Studer explains. "They also give us an opportunity to recognize employees who receive positive comments on the survey."

❧ *Employee performance.* To increase accountability in the organization, all Baptist's leaders and middle managers get "report cards" every 90 days. "That's how we align behavior to our goals and how we can reward objectively, which takes politics out of the game," says Studer. These "report cards" typically measure performance in four areas. "One is customer service; we measure it against our goal, which is to be in the top 1% of hospitals in the country," Studer says. "All the employees know what will satisfy our customers and where our weaknesses lie, because they know the results of the patient-satisfaction survey." The other three scores on the report card monitor the manager's efficiency, expense management, and success at keeping employee turnover low. "Everyone's got a turnover goal based on his or her unit and its past history," Studer explains. "Twenty percent of my incentive compensation is based on employee turnover. That gets my attention."

❧ *Employee satisfaction.* To reduce employee turnover and its associated costs, Baptist measures employee satisfaction as much as it tracks customer satisfaction. To get a handle on morale, the hospital *(Continued)*

(Continued from page 169)

holds company forums for employees every 90 days and regularly surveys them about their satisfaction with their jobs and workplace. "We used the same sort of survey tool to measure employee satisfaction that we'd used to measure customer satisfaction. We found out that the biggest thing that bugged our employees was that their evaluations were late. They want feedback," Studer observes. "Employees also want supervisors who accept their input with respect and appreciation. They want to know about matters that affect them."

After just two years—in an environment in which hospital admissions are static or going down—Baptist's admissions were up 8.3%, and outpatient volume was up 33%. As for patient satisfaction, Baptist ranked number two in the country for all hospitals and number one for hospitals with more than 100 beds. Employee satisfaction had improved 30%, and physician satisfaction had risen from 72.4% to 81.3%. Job turnover for nurses went from 30% to 18%.

Despite his emphasis on setting goals and measuring results, Studer believes that a leader's personal commitment matters, too. "You have to really believe in what you're doing," he says. "When I got to Baptist, I said, 'We're going to be the best hospital in the country,' and somebody said, 'Quint, you mean county.' I said, 'No, I mean country.' You have to decide what you want to do, act on that decision, and look at the results."

93
IDEA

Doing Well by Doing Good

More and more entrepreneurial companies are recognizing that support of employees' community service work can help those employees feel better about their jobs and their companies. Not long ago, Jenai Lane, president of Respect Inc., a San Francisco company with 1998 revenues of $2 million, launched a new initiative. **Employees get paid for doing volunteer work**. One day a month, each of Respect's 10 employees can work at a nonprofit of his or her choice, and Lane will pay the employee for the time.

Lane, whose company manufactures jewelry, cosmetics, and accessories, began the program when she realized how busy her employees' lives were. She says, "I think it really helps with employee morale and giving people a sense of purpose."

While some entrepreneurs follow Lane's route and encourage employees to pursue their own interests, other companies try to involve workers in community-service projects related to the business. For example, Kay Hirai, owner of a Seattle hair salon called Studio 904, takes her 22 employees, including 13 stylists, to an elementary school in a low-income neighborhood each month to cut children's hair.

Other companies offer a mix of employee involvement and company giving. In 1992, Jim Dodson, president of an Indianapolis collective that buys office services such as supplies and overnight delivery services, started the Sycamore Foundation. The foundation consolidated the Dodson Group's support of several social-service organizations. "This way, we can give even when the company has a down year," says Dodson, whose company gives 10% of its after-tax profits to the foundation.   *(Continued)*

(Continued from page 171)

The foundation then underwrites an annual charity golf marathon, and Dodson Group employees help out on the day of the event. The foundation allows selected nonprofit organizations to use the event as a fundraiser by charging people to play. That way, Dodson says, the company's giving is leveraged and multiplied. While the event costs about $15,000, the nonprofits raise about $40,000.

Meanwhile, on the fourth Friday of each month, Dodson Group employees serve at the local soup kitchen on company-paid time. Dodson finds that the program, which has been in place since the early 1990s, is good for employee morale and attitude. The stint at the soup kitchen gives employees a reprieve from their hectic jobs, plus some needed perspective. "A lot of our people work in customer service, and they hear about problems all day long," says Dodson, whose company reported 1998 revenues of $11 million. After three hours of serving food to homeless people, they realize that "the problems we have with customer complaints are not really a problem at all."

94
IDEA

Value System

Bob Dabic remembers that in the old days, it wasn't much fun to manage his workforce. "I got frustrated with all the little fires and personality problems," recalls the president of Dabico, a 50-employee airport-equipment manufacturer.

Today, Dabic says, his job as company president is much easier, because his company, which is based in Costa Mesa, Calif., has articulated its values and outlined the type of behavior it exemplifies. With clearly defined corporate values, Dabic finds that conflicts within the company occur less frequently and are more easily resolved. "It prevents problems, and when problems occur, you get an understanding much more quickly," he says. "We now all kind of know what the agenda is."

One of the company's stated values, for example, is "teamwork." If one team refuses to help another team, someone might point out that such behavior doesn't fit the company's values. "The beauty of it is the accountability to which everyone is held," Dabic says. "It has revolutionized the management of people."

That revolution didn't come easily, however. Dabic says he began the transition to **value-based leadership** in the early 1990s. The whole management team developed a company vision statement, and then Dabic himself articulated the company's five overarching "Vision Values"—making customers happy, satisfying employees, helping others, growing net profits, and exhibiting teamwork.

While Dabic came up with those values for his company, he left it to the staff to develop detailed plans for implementing them. As *(Continued)*

(Continued from page 173)

he explains it, each general value also includes three bullet points detailing how the value will be put into practice—and the staff creates those bullet points. For example, to implement the Dabico value of helping others, the company has started allowing employees two hours a week to volunteer in the community on company time.

In addition to its overall Vision Values, the company also has what Dabic calls operational or cultural values, which the management team developed or adapted from existing company policy. Operational values include things like the company's quality policy and its emphasis on rapid responsiveness to customer needs.

&. Dabic credits the emphasis on company values with helping to double sales between 1993 and 1998—and more than doubling profits. He admits the process was very difficult, but he believes it was well worth the struggle. "It's a three- to five-year plan that's a very painful transition," Dabic says. But once that transition is over, "you'll never go back." Dabic compares his management-by-values system to something "approaching cruise control" for a business. "It guides people in helping them to do more of the right things more of the time," Dabic observes.

95
IDEA

Stop, Thief!

Entrepreneur David Schulhof never imagined that one of his own workers would rip him off. Until, that is, an accounting manager he hired at a company he owned bilked him out of approximately $200,000 within two months. The employee, Schulhof says, fraudulently changed the company's check-signing card at the bank to require his signature alone. Then he began writing checks almost daily to his own account. "I should have caught it," admits Schulhof, who says he was too busy managing a fast-growing business to read bank statements.

Schulhof eventually sold that company, but he has learned to do things differently. At his next company, Schulhof outsourced accounting and signed all checks himself. He assigned one employee to do accounts receivable and another to do accounts payable, because, he reasoned, it's less likely that two employees will conspire against the company. And, with prospective hires' permission, Schulhof started running personal credit checks. "I don't care if they missed a mortgage payment two years ago," he says. Instead he looked for larger discrepancies.

Schulhof is not the only entrepreneur to experience employee theft. According to a study prepared by the Association of Certified Fraud Examiners, in Austin, Tex., small companies are especially vulnerable to theft because small firms apply fewer controls, and people tend to trust those whom they think they know well.

What should Schulhof have done to **set up safeguards against internal theft**? For one thing, he should have read his bank statements, says Joseph T. Wells, chairman of the association. "What do you think he   *(Continued)*

(Continued from page 175)

would have seen?" asks Wells. "All these checks payable to his employee." Here are some other precautions from Wells:

🦂 *Make it known that all monthly bank statements will always be delivered, unopened, to your desk.* "Let everyone know you're going to look through every deposit and every check," says Wells. "But do it nicely."

🦂 *Keep an eye out for statement discrepancies.* "Look for unusual patterns and unfamiliar vendors or financial trends. Take, for example, checks made payable to companies you don't recognize, or dual endorsements. One way to convert a check is to take a check made payable to someone else and add a name so it's payable to both people. Or, if there are two signatures, one could be a forgery."

🦂 *Divvy up financial tasks.* "In a small business, the person who keeps the books should not be the same person who keeps the money. If you have only one person, the boss ought at least to be signing the checks."

IX

"When someone leaves, you definitely lose something, but you also gain an opportunity to re-create that position."

LAURA HENDERSON
president, CEO, and founder,
Prospect Associates, Silver Spring, Md.

IDEA

Downtime Is Not a "Downer"

Does your company's workload have seasonal fluctuations? Lancaster Laboratories, an analytical-services company in Lancaster, Pa., has developed an **alternative to seasonal layoffs**. Lancaster has an environmental division whose business is slow from January through March, when winter conditions make it difficult to take water and soil samples. Instead of laying off workers, the company has a formal arrangement with a local temp agency to provide about a dozen affected employees with work in the off months. The employees work for the agency but stay on Lancaster's payroll and keep their benefits. Lancaster Laboratories, which had 1998 sales of $40 million, gets back most of the costs from the temp agency. "It's worth it because of the cost of training new people," says Carol Hess, Lancaster's executive vice-president of administrative services. "In 37 years, we've never laid anyone off for lack of work."

Avoiding Layoffs

No matter how hard you try, you can't always predict your revenues. So, what do you do when sales don't materialize and you're suddenly facing an unanticipated downturn? How do you balance your company's need to retain talented and loyal employees with the need to cut costs? Every situation varies, but here are several **creative alternatives to laying off employees**.

If you can afford it, use the downturn to work on long-term projects. During a six-month lull, Bob Dabic, president and CEO of Dabico, in Costa Mesa, Calif., put teams of employees to work on internal improvement projects. Thanks to a cash cushion, the airport-equipment manufacturer, which has about 50 employees, was able to use the slow period to revamp important business processes. Dabic also kept some workers busy renovating the plant.

Ask employees for suggestions. That's what April Morris, president of Associated Engineers, in Ontario, Calif., did some years ago when work slowed at her civil-engineering company, which had 1998 revenues of close to $4 million. Morris explained the company's situation and asked the engineers for ideas. One result: Twelve salaried engineers volunteered to take an hourly wage for a while, getting paid only when they had billable work. The voluntary cutback helped, but Morris still had to make some tough decisions: She let three engineers go and switched three others to part-time. Six months later, however, the 12 volunteers got their salaries back.

Ask employees to work part-time. A cash-flow crisis in *(Continued)*

(Continued from page 179)

the mid-1990s left few options open to Sales Building Systems, a database marketing company in Mentor, Ohio. To survive, CEO Tim McCarthy turned many full-time positions into part-time jobs and let 13 people go. Over time, he replaced the departed employees with two kinds of part-timers: those who work part-time by preference and those who ultimately want full-time work.

According to McCarthy, the new arrangement has made the company, which had sales of $4.2 million in 1998, more agile. Now the company relies heavily on part-timers. During down periods, McCarthy says, the company first asks for volunteers who may want more time off. If that doesn't reduce payroll enough, the company can begin reducing part-timers' hours across the board. Most new hires now start part-time, and almost all full-time recruiting is done internally.

McCarthy finds that the workers who are attracted to part-time jobs form an interesting workforce—and a talented one. "The person who runs the company started as a part-timer," he notes. Meanwhile, McCarthy keeps morale up by sharing 10% of profits with everyone on staff—20 full-time employees and 20 to 40 part-timers. Profit-sharing is apportioned by hours worked.

98 IDEA

Please Don't Go

A few years ago, Eric Rabinowitz, president of IHS Helpdesk Service—a company that supplies on-site contract workers to staff technical-support lines at *Fortune* 500 companies—discovered that his firm desperately needed to **reduce turnover**. Working a help desk can be thankless and full of pressure, since callers are often impatient about getting their problems resolved. For this reason, the average annual turnover rate in the help-desk industry was at least 50%. Rabinowitz discovered, however, that annual turnover at IHS was approaching 300%! What's more, 30% of new hires at IHS weren't staying three months.

Rabinowitz and Séan Durham, president of Leveraged Technology, the New York City-based parent company of IHS, calculated that it cost the company $3,000 a head to bring on new hires. If they could nudge their average employee's tenure from 3.5 months to just 3.8 months, they would save $60,000. Get the average up to 7 months, and they'd recover $275,000. And that wasn't including the indirect cost of turnover, such as accompanying decreases in customer satisfaction.

IHS needed to attack several problems. One was the fact that most IHS help-desk staffers worked at customers' sites. Naturally, they felt more a part of the customer's culture than IHS's. So Rabinowitz created *IHS Weekly Helpings*, a newsletter that has been faxed to all employees every week since 1997. It offers technical tips and information about the company's various programs and incentives, along with trivia, quotes, and contests.

IHS has also created a new tier of employees, called account managers, whose job is to nurture the company's relationships with *(Continued)*

(Continued from page 181)

both clients and its remote employees. An account manager may place regular calls to each of IHS's field employees to keep them abreast of new policies, ask them whether they are going to the company picnic, or even just say a quick hello. The account managers also make visits to the customer sites and can touch base with the IHS employees there. This helps IHS staffers put a face or, at the very least, a voice on their formerly invisible employer.

After studying the numbers, Rabinowitz concluded that any employee who took part in any of IHS's training programs stayed with the company an average of two years. Meanwhile, any employee who didn't participate in a training program stayed less than half of that time. The impact of training, says Rabinowitz, is "just incredible." As a result, the company has tripled the amount it spends on employee training. Currently, Rabinowitz says, some 60% of employees participate in IHS's training programs, but he would like to see that number reach 85%.

In a further effort to forge a bond with employees, IHS now holds mandatory one-day paid group orientation sessions for new employees working out of the company's New York office. Those sessions include a tour of Madison Square Garden, and Rabinowitz says he attends every one of these orientations.

The multipronged approach at IHS has worked. In 1996, Rabinowitz reports that turnover actually ended up at 115%, not 300%. In 1997, turnover dropped to 65%, a number closer to the industry average. And by the first quarter of 1999, Rabinowitz says that IHS's turnover was running at 23% and that the average employee tenure was up to a year, rather than 3.5 months. Meanwhile, in fiscal 1998, IHS's sales grew to $15 million, while its parent company, Leveraged Technology, reported revenues of $23 million.

See You in Court

Some companies deserve to be sued by an employee for wrongful termination, but a disturbing number of companies are victims of frivolous lawsuits initiated by employees eager to jump on the litigation bandwagon. Three CEOs who have felt **the sting of wrongful-termination lawsuits** tell what they learned from the experience.

   ❧ *Don't settle automatically.* Many companies handle wrongful-termination suits the easy way. Guilty or not, they settle out of court. But Stephen Swinson, president of the technology division of Trigen Energy Corp., thinks that strategy can be disastrous. "You send a message to employees that all they have to do is write a threatening letter and they'll get a check," says Swinson, whose company is based in Kansas City, Mo. "Provided you're right, you have to go through with the litigation." Trigen was sued in the mid-1990s by an employee who was fired for poor performance but claimed he was terminated for reporting a labor-law violation. Although Swinson might have spared himself considerable headaches by settling, he went to court, instead. The case, which Trigen won, took six months and cost $10,000 in lawyers' fees. But, says Swinson, "it was absolutely worth it because of the message it sent."

   ❧ *Create written policies.* Six years ago George Woelper, president of Lincoln Tile Co., in Marietta, Ga., which had 1998 revenues of $6.5 million, fired an employee for insubordination after the company had given him repeated oral and written warnings. Claiming that he had been terminated without cause, the employee filed a complaint with the state Department of Labor and demanded that the company pay *(Continued)*

(Continued from page 183)

him full unemployment benefits. "We thought we had a simple case," says Woelper. But to his dismay, the DOL agreed with the employee, a decision that cost the company $10,000 in legal fees and higher insurance premiums. The rationale? The DOL noted that Lincoln Tile had no formal written policy citing insubordination as just cause for termination. It does now. Woelper requires all employees to sign a document that spells out the penalties for bad behavior such as drug use, tardiness, and, yes, insubordination. He feels confident that the agreement, which employees helped create, will shield him against future litigation. "We haven't had a problem since," Woelper says.

❧ *Stay alert.* The CEO of a small California electronics manufacturer, who asked not to be identified, has spent $100,000 defending against a suit from a senior manager who quit, apparently over some organizational changes. The former manager then sued the company for wrongful termination. The CEO says the manager was "an excellent performer but caused a lot of trouble among employees with harsh, rude behavior." The CEO now realizes that he valued the manager's technical expertise so much that he ignored his predilection for troublemaking. "When we first saw the difficulties he had interacting with people, I should have asked employees to document their complaints in writing, and I should have issued a written warning," he says. From now on, he will.

No Vacancy

When you lose an employee, your first reaction may be: Whom shall I hire or promote? Most of the time, that's the right question. But it also pays to ask: **Do I really need a replacement for that person?** Consider the case of Leonhardt Plating Co., a metal-finishing company in Cincinnati with revenues of $2 million.

After the death of his polishing foreman, CEO Daniel Leonhardt decided not to hire a new foreman. Instead, he let the polishing department rule itself by committee. Leonhardt reasoned that the five people in the department are very experienced, and the work is "a craft," unlike work done by production employees. A foreman from another department handles scheduling for the polishing department, Leonhardt says, but the polishing employees themselves decide who will do which job. There have been "no major problems" with the arrangement, says Leonhardt. "It has worked out pretty well."

Clearing the Air

Firings are difficult—for the person dismissed, for the manager who gives the employee the word, and for the remaining employees—especially at small companies where everyone knows each other. That's why president Jenai Lane **doesn't let a firing go undiscussed at her company**, Respect Inc., in San Francisco.

Like most businesspeople, Lane doesn't relish the idea of firing an employee. After she lets someone go at her close-knit, 10-person office, Lane holds what she calls an emergency powwow. She asks employees to say what's on their minds about the dismissal. "It takes a little prodding, but it's good to get people's feelings out in the open," says Lane, whose company—which has revenues of $2 million—produces jewelry, accessories, and cosmetics.

Lane also tries to avoid firing anyone by keeping employees on track. To help employees understand what's expected, she writes job descriptions for new workers and switches from quarterly reviews to monthly reviews if employees fail to meet job requirements.

Other business books from *Inc.*

FINANCIAL TROUBLESHOOTING:
AN ACTION PLAN FOR MONEY MANAGEMENT
IN SMALL AND GROWING BUSINESSES
By David H. Bangs, Jr., and Michael Pellecchia

THE NEXT LEVEL:
ESSENTIAL STRATEGIES FOR ACHIEVING
BREAKTHROUGH GROWTH
By James B. Wood, with Larry Rothstein

HOW TO *REALLY* CREATE A SUCCESSFUL BUSINESS PLAN
HOW TO *REALLY* CREATE A SUCCESSFUL MARKETING PLAN
HOW TO *REALLY* START YOUR OWN BUSINESS
By David E. Gumpert

MANAGING PEOPLE:
HOW TO *REALLY* RECRUIT, MOTIVATE, AND LEAD YOUR TEAM
Edited by Ruth G. Newman
with Bradford W. Ketchum, Jr.

HOW TO *REALLY* DELIVER SUPERIOR CUSTOMER SERVICE
Edited by John Halbrooks

THE SERVICE BUSINESS PLANNING GUIDE
THE GUIDE TO RETAIL BUSINESS PLANNING
By Warren G. Purdy

Inc.'s "301" series:

301 GREAT IDEAS FOR SELLING SMARTER
FROM AMERICA'S MOST INNOVATIVE SMALL COMPANIES
Edited by Teri Lammers Prior, with Jacqueline Lapidus

301 GREAT IDEAS FOR USING TECHNOLOGY
FROM AMERICA'S MOST INNOVATIVE SMALL COMPANIES
Edited by Phaedra Hise

301 GREAT CUSTOMER SERVICE IDEAS
FROM AMERICA'S MOST INNOVATIVE SMALL COMPANIES
Edited by Nancy Artz

301 DO-IT-YOURSELF MARKETING IDEAS
FROM AMERICA'S MOST INNOVATIVE SMALL COMPANIES
Edited by Sam Decker

301 GREAT MANAGEMENT IDEAS
FROM AMERICA'S MOST INNOVATIVE SMALL COMPANIES
Edited by Leslie Brokaw

Langdon Public Library
328 Nimble Hill Road
Newington, NH 03801
603-436-5154
www.langdonlibrary.org

www.inc.com

To receive a complete listing of *Inc.* business books and videos, please call 1-800-468-0800, ext. 5505.
Or write to *Inc.* Business Resources, P.O. Box 1365, Dept. 5505, Wilkes-Barre, PA 18703-1365